'Getting Ready for Love' is like getting advice from your favourite uncle who understands the times and knows how to talk to you in a way that you'll get it. It's a great book; a light and easy read for such a heavy topic. As I was reading it, there was a list in my mind of all the people I would recommend the book to, and the list kept growing. I've been married for nine years, Alhamdulillah, and I found many gems in the book; things I've known but forgotten, things I've never thought about, and things that are just refreshing to read. It's peppered with practical advice, backed up by people who know their stuff. Sheikh Rakin reminds us that finding "the right person" is important, but what's also important is *you* being (or becoming) "the right person." We are reminded to be self-aware, to work towards self-improvement and spiritual nourishment. We are reminded that marriage is a partnership; it's two people navigating the joys and travails of life together, growing towards Allah. We are reminded that it is all for God, and that following the way of our beloved Prophet Muhammad (PBUH) will lead us closer to God and fill our lives with blessings. We are reminded that companionship laced with good intentions, knowledge, preparation and Trust in Allah is a beautiful thing. I really recommend this book and strongly believe that it should be on every bookshelf. Whether you're single, getting ready for marriage, married or divorced, this book is for you!

Sajida Mohammed, Editor and Children's Book Author

Getting Ready For Love is a must-read Islamic marriage guide. Written by a UK-trained life coach and relationship expert with years of marital and counselling experience, the book provides insightful guidance on anyone seeking a loving, committed relationship. Full of wisdom from the Islamic tradition on how to get married and improve intimacy, the book is supplemented with scientific research to help you develop emotional intimacy and emotional intelligence. Whether you are married or looking for a spouse, Rakin Niass provides practical advice on the complexities of modern-day marriage and finding love after divorce. A well-researched and recommended read for Muslim men and women.

Habeeb Akande, author of A Taste of Honey

I really enjoyed reading this book, it was thought-provoking and is easy to read and understand by young millennials who are approaching the age of marriage. As a coach and therapist, I cannot emphasise how crucial it is for people to be educated on the purpose and beauty of marriage in Islam. I regularly work with people who did not take much of the advice given in this book when they got married and they fell into abusive and turbulent relationships. I'd like to add to Ustadh Rakin's work the importance of going to therapy before searching for a partner, so that one does not take their previous issues into the marriage; expecting their partner to deal with them. This adds a heavy strain to the marriage that is unable to start strong. I have had the pleasure of collaborating with Ustadh Rakin before, and mashallah he is a great example of a Muslim family man. I hope this book gets distributed in all Islamic bookshops; may Allah place a lot of blessings and rewards in it. Ameen!

Dr. Mona Alyedreessy, author of The Muslim Narcissist

This is a relationship book needed on every shelf. Anyone concerned with their deen and their life partner (whether married already or not yet) must read this book to put them in the best position for achieving a loving, long-lasting and understanding relationship, the one you were always meant to have. As the book says, it does take work to build a meaningful relationship but equipped with the knowledge contained in this book, it will be worthwhile and satisfying. Allah says 'Ask the people of remembrance if you do not know'. Many of us aren't taught what makes a good relationship and here you have the ingredients to make it so.

Sekina Yakub, author of Hearts Connect

A truly insightful and practical self-help guide for anyone who is looking to meet someone for marriage and start the next chapter of their lives. 'Getting Ready for Love' takes the reader on a step by step journey starting from what the Quran and Sunnah say about marriage, to doing the inner work, to what to consider when looking for a partner and the best approach to take when speaking to someone for marriage. It is a good reminder of how to approach the subject of marriage within an Islamic framework and values. This book caters to all seeking a life partner – even if you have been married before and are looking to settle down once again!

Nazra Zuhyle, Life Coach and Storyteller

GETTING READY FOR LOVE

A GUIDE TO COMPLETING HALF YOUR DEEN

RAKIN FETUGA

Getting Ready for Love: A Guide to Completing Half Your Deen

First published 2024
Al Lateef Publishing
Copyright © Rakin Fetuga
All rights reserved.

website: sunlightlifecoaching.com
email: sunlightlifecoaching@gmail.com
instagram: sunlightlifecoaching
tiktok: Coachrakin

ISBN:978-1-9993461-1-1-9

Cover design by: Amina Ofori

DEDICATION

Dedicating this book to my dear wife, Adwoa Amina, thank you for all of your love, kindness and companionship over all of these years. Thank you for also giving me four wonderful children: Dr.Kamal, Rakaya, Shafiq and Junayd.

CONTENTS

INTRODUCTION

Love is like a flower: it needs water, it needs sunshine, it needs attention. Gardeners often say that plants grow better when you talk to them. They need attention. You have to look after them, cut the leaves, remove dead leaves and make sure the soil is also firm. It needs to be watered regularly, you can't just water it once. It needs constant attention. If you do all of these things, then your plant will blossom.

Relationships are just like the plant, they need constant work and attention. It's important to always do actions that will show your love and appreciation for them. Why many relationships go wrong is because people stop working on their relationship. Often, they have the wrong understanding. They believe that just being in the same house, sleeping

1

in the same bed and paying all the bills is enough, but sadly it isn't. With guidance from the Qur'an and Sunna and my own personal experience, this book provides a helpful framework for being successful in finding love and having a healthy relationship with your partner.

It was narrated from Abu Hurairah that the Messenger of Allah (ﷺ) said:

> "*Marry, for I will boast of your great numbers.*" (Ibn Majah)

Getting Ready for Love

This self-help book prepares you for the massive step of marriage in Islam. In today's ever-changing society there is a lot of confusion around marriage.

Many people question why they should get married when everything that takes place within a marriage can be done outside of it.

With the advancement of capitalism and atheism, we find ourselves in a situation where the concept of God is dwindling out of the picture, so people's values are created based on how things make them feel. Therefore, the idea of 'as long as it doesn't hurt anybody, it's all okay' is prevalent. This leads to a culture of sex outside of marriage being perceived as a norm, leading to the concept of marriage becoming defunct and outdated.

3

WHAT IS THE CHALLENGE?

People are not getting married as much as they once did. In today's society we find many amazing men and women who are not getting married. I have many wonderful friends of both sexes that are not married, and they are really great people who have so much to offer. But even though this is the case, they are not taking the step of getting married.

This challenge is not only a western problem. We find Muslims all over the world who are finding difficulties in meeting their other half and tying the knot. The interesting thing about this situation is that men and women do meet each other a lot, but mostly as friends or as part of a large friendship group. Although they have this chance to meet, many of them find it difficult to transition out of the friendship zone into a relationship which leads to marriage.

The other issue is how to behave within a relationship. In Islam it is a cultural norm for men and women not to mix. Mixing is generally accepted for education, when you are with your family or in the workplace.

This is generally more of an issue in Muslim

countries, however even in western countries you can find men and women growing up 'within certain communities' who have no real experience of socialising with the opposite sex. This is a massive problem because marriage is a whole new arena where you need knowledge of how to operate in that space. Many marriages are taking place where the couple have no idea of what it takes being in a marriage.

This leads to unhappy marriages and in many cases, divorce. The divorce rate amongst Muslims is growing. According to the 2021 Census by the Office for National Statistics, divorce rates in the UK are at 42%.

This book will give you a rounded understanding of marriage, what to expect and how you should behave with your spouse. It will also give you tools that you can use in your marriage to help sustain a healthy and fruitful one.

Marriage is not easy; it is a journey of discovery, but with knowledge about the different kinds of tests and challenges that can occur in marriage, this will go a long way in assisting your preparation.

MY STORY

I am happily married and have been married for over three decades. I have been blessed with four amazing children and I am trying my best to bring them up to be four brilliant individuals who will hopefully be wholesome adults and positive assets to society.

I studied Sociology at Roehampton University and went on to do my Postgraduate in Social and Emotional Behavioural Difficulties. I also completed a Post Graduate in Education and have been a secondary school teacher since 2005.

A few years ago, alongside my teaching, I trained as a life coach and have been specialising in relationship coaching, and practice solution-focused therapy. I have found that there are multiple issues in the Muslim community.

One of the biggest areas is that Muslims are not really preparing themselves for marriage. There are many Muslims that are getting married everyday but the work that needs to be put in before marriage is not being done. I'm happy to see this is changing now, and I am witnessing, in many cases, young Muslims taking courses on marriage. This will go a long way to change the present challenges we are facing as a community. Gone are the days when a Muslim woman would be happy to just be married. In the past they needed to rely on men for their livelihoods. Today's women are more independent and expect a fantastic relationship; where their spouse shows them that they appreciate them and works hard on their relationship to make sure it is rich and meaningful.

I was inspired to write this book because I realised that there is a breakdown in marriages, leading to divorce, and that less people are getting married. Through my experience of having conversations with both males and females, I realised there is a gap in connections. Men and women are not able to have deep conversations and this is something that is necessary to build deep and strong relationships. In the Muslim community, I found that people can get distracted by finding the right hadiths (sayings of the Prophet) instead of connecting with the person in front of them.

I have been married for over 30 years to a wonderful woman and have learned so much about what it takes to have a strong and loving relationship.

Marriage is not an easy game; it is a journey where lessons are constantly learnt, it is something that needs to be worked on. The best marriages are the ones that both partners actively work on improving. One of the most important areas in a marriage is communication. It needs to be fluid and constant. A large proportion of the issues that arise in marriages are connected to poor communication.

HOW IS THIS BOOK GOING TO HELP YOU?

This book will help you get prepared for a loving relationship. It will let you know if you are ready for a relationship by showing you what a loving partnership entails. It will also help you prepare yourself spiritually, emotionally and psychologically for the next stage of your life.

Getting Ready for Love will give you a clear understanding about what the challenges are and why they are here. It will also empower you with knowledge, which will enable you to move past the problem and start meeting potential spouses.

The hope is to educate the seeker on how to choose the correct spouse. Many people looking for love have no idea what they are looking for in a spouse. That is usually because they have no idea what their needs are. Usually, there is a lot of pressure around getting married which can come from friends and family, but it is better to choose the right partner than to just rush and get married to the first person that comes along. Remember, haste is from the Shaytan and it will benefit you immensely if you know yourself well and also know what you want in your partner.

This book will explain the beneficial characteristics that you should be looking for in a partner. For example, beauty is important but what is more important is beauty of the soul, and the latter takes a longer time to be able to identify.

How will you be able to be a good, loving partner if you don't understand the needs of your spouse?

This book will help you understand what marriage is about and the key roles for all partners in the marriage.

This book will also inform you of the challenges that exist in society around marriage. It will explain the main reasons why men and women are not getting married as much as they once did, why both sexes are more selective about their partners and why many women are making sure they educate themselves to degree level before they start searching for a marriage partner.

This book will also equip you with knowledge that will help to support your marriage and make it blossom. It will give you knowledge on things to practice inside your marriage so both partners will enjoy being married. It will help you to un 1derstand why so many marriages fail and the traps to watch out for.

You will gain a deeper insight into what the Qur'an says about marriage and also what the Prophet Muhammad (ﷺ) said about marriage.

There are many Muslims who think they are following the Sunna in marriage, but they are not. The Prophet of Islam (ﷺ) said in a famous hadith:

> "*The best of you are the ones that are best to your wives and I am best to my wives.*"

10

The Importance of Intention

As Muslims, it's important to start everything with a pure intention.

Our intention is to worship Allah, as He (SWT) has created us to worship Him. Marriage is part of worship; Allah wants us to be with our partners to find love and happiness in this world; to find companionship, support and partnership on this journey called life. A good partner will benefit you a great deal and will make your journey on this earth easy and enjoyable.

It all starts with having the correct intention in the beginning. If your aim is to find a beautiful person, that is okay. But it is better to find a beautiful person that loves Allah and loves the Prophet Muhammad

(ﷺ) and tries their best to live a life according to the teachings of Islam.

It is narrated on the authority of Amir al-Mu'minin (Leader of the Believers), Abu Hafs 'Umar bin al-Khattab (may Allah be pleased with him), who said:

> "*I heard the messenger of Allah (peace be upon him), say:*
>
> *Actions are according to intentions, and everyone will get what was intended. Whoever migrates with an intention for Allah and His messenger, the migration will be for the sake of Allah and His messenger. And whoever migrates for worldly gain or to marry a woman, then his migration will be for the sake of whatever he migrated for.*"
> (Bukhari & Muslim)

This hadith explains clearly the importance of having intentions before all of our actions. As Muslims, our main intention should be to please Allah and we do this by worshipping Him. As Allah states:

"And I did not create the jinn and mankind except to worship Me." (Quran, 51:56)

You will get whatever you intend; so when making your intention for a partner, make the intention of finding a partner that will make your life in worshipping Allah easier. If you have this, then I guarantee you that you will have a life of bliss.

Why do I say this? It is because life is not a straightforward road; it has many bumps and rough roads. Sometimes the roads are straight and smooth, but oftentimes they are rough with many potholes. For you to be able to get through this challenge of the rough roads, you will need a partner that will help to guide you through those rough terrains. An example of this can be the loss of a job; now this is an extreme situation for anyone.

Many marriages fail because of a partner losing their job and then not being able to offer their partner the lifestyle they are used to. This can lead to increased pressure on the marriage for both parties. The person who has lost their job can be filled with anger and self-doubt and also a dip in self-confidence. They may start questioning themselves

– 'why did I lose the job?'; 'It's my fault, I should have been working harder.'

The partner may be filled with fear and worry. This may happen because of fear of debt which could lead to the couple losing their house or flat. Tensions will rise in this situation, which could lead to arguments between the couple. Now this situation could have been much better if both parties involved took a different perspective on the situation. If both parties saw the situation as a test from Allah, this would invoke different responses. Instead of being filled with fear and worry, the person would turn to Allah in Dua. We have been taught by our beloved Prophet (ﷺ) that Dua is the weapon of the believer.

Allah (SWT) says in the Qur'an:

"Our Lord! Shower us with perseverance, and let us die while submitting (to You)." (7:126)

It was reported that the Prophet (ﷺ) used to recite this Dua:

اللّٰهُمَّ رَحْمَتَكَ أَرْجُو فَلَا تَكِلْنِي إِلَى نَفْسِي طَرْفَةَ عَيْنٍ، وَأَصْلِحْ لِي شَأْنِي كُلَّهُ لَا إِلٰهَ إِلَّا أَنْتَ

14

"O Allah, I hope for Your mercy. Do not leave me to myself even for the blinking of an eye (i.e. a moment). Correct all of my affairs for me. There is none worthy of worship but You." (Abu Dawud 4/324, Ahmad 5/42. Al-Albani graded it as good in Sahih Abu Dawud 3/959)

When you are planning to get married, make sure to purify your intention. The first reason should be to find a life partner that is going to help and support you on your path to Allah. Once your intention is focused on Allah then success will be your end.

In the chapter on marriage in Imam Ghazali's famous book 'Revival of the Religious Sciences', he explains that the Prophet Muhammad (ﷺ) said:

"Marriage is of my Sunna; whoever refrains from my Sunna refrains from me"; and he also said: "Marriage is of my Sunna; whoever likes my fitrah (natural disposition),' let him follow my Sunna."

"Marry and multiply for I will boast

about you over other nations on the day of resurrection, even about the least among you."

"Whoever refrains from my Sunna, he is not of me, and marriage is part of my Sunna; whoever loves me, let him follow my Sunna."

All of these quotes from the Prophet Muhammad (ﷺ) indicate how much importance the Prophet placed on marriage. Marriage is the centrepiece of Islam; from it comes families and families develop into communities.

Imam Ghazali quotes from many of the companions of the Prophet (ﷺ) regarding what they said about marriage:

> Ibn 'Abbas* said: "The asceticism of an ascetic is not complete until he marries." It is possible that he considered marriage an act of devotion which renders asceticism perfect; but it seems that he meant to say thereby that the heart would not be safe from being overcome by desire except through

marriage, and that asceticism is not perfect without emptying (faragh) the heart [of all preoccupations].

This is where it is clear to see that Islam sees marriage differently than other faiths. It is a must for spiritual advancement, it is a protection against committing *haram*. In the Catholic church the priests do not get married, the idea is that they are married to God and they also use the argument that Jesus was never married. But in Islam, it is clear that it is a must if you can and a great blessing.

Here are some good examples of how the companions of the Prophet Muhammad (ﷺ) took marriage very seriously:

Ibn Masud used to say, "Were there but ten days left of my life, I would be inclined to get married so as not to meet God a celibate."

When two of Mu'adh Ibn Jabal's wives died from the plague, and he, too, was afflicted with the plague; he said, "Get me married, for I would not like to meet God a celibate."

And this coming from both of them indicates that they considered marriage a virtue rather than a defence against the excessiveness of desire.

WHAT DOES THE QUR'AN SAY ABOUT IT?

"Do not prevent them from marrying their husbands when they agree between themselves in a lawful manner."

(Qur'an 2:232)

In the Qur'an it expresses the importance of marriage in Islam. It is clear that marriage is the foundation of Islam because this is where families are formed and where children are born into. We know that the first place of socialisation for the person is at home with their family or carers. This is also where they learn about themselves and their faith; the first teachers being the parents, before they go to school to learn further.

Marriage is so important in Islam, as the Prophet (ﷺ) explained; there are two ways the faith of Islam spreads: one is through Muslims having children and bringing them up on the path and the second way is by people converting to Islam.

It's important for parents to work with their children when it comes to marriage. The children have the right to agree on who they marry. So even in the case of an arranged marriage, where parents choose the spouse, the son or daughter has the right to agree or disagree with the parent's choice.

When this kind of agreement is present in a family it will lead to justice and a happier marriage. Parents can guide and advise their child but ultimately it is the son or daughter's choice; this is because it is them that will be living with the person.

Parents should not try to force their son or daughter to marry anyone; this is against the teachings of Islam. The parent can only suggest, guide and advise, but the final choice should be with the son/daughter. I have heard cases where parents have one person in mind for their daughter, so they refuse many suitable suitors because they want their daughter to marry their person.

This is very wrong and is *haram* (forbidden). It is paramount that the child's opinions are heard and respected. Forced marriages are against the teachings of Islam and do not lead to happy marriages. There are many cases where the son/daughter marries a person just to please the family, then after a year or so they divorce the person and go on to marry their desired choice of spouse.

> *"Women of purity are for men of purity, and men of purity are for women of purity."* (Qur'an, 24:26)

This ayat gives an idea of who someone should marry. A person should look for someone who is on their level. Someone who has the same likes as them and someone who has a similar understanding of the deen as them. This is also very important for a smooth running of the relationship. If a couple have nothing at all in common, this can lead to many concerns and problems in the relationship. Your spouse is not only your marriage partner, they are your best friend; a person that understands your dreams and goals and works with you to reach your goals.

From this verse we can also infer that women that are virgins would be good for men that are the same. Due to their non-experience in the bedroom, they would be able to grow together. Sometimes, if one partner is more experienced sexually than the other partner (e.g. been married before) this could cause issues in the marriage. The other partner may feel pressured or insecure when it comes to love making.

This is not always the case though; our beloved Prophet Muhammad (ﷺ) married his first wife, Sayyida Khadija (RA) and she was a widow, so she had been married before, but this did not affect their marriage. The Prophet (ﷺ) loved her the most out of all of his wives and while he was with Khadija (RA) he never married any other woman.

> "*Men are in charge of women by [right of] what Allah has given one over the other and what they spend [for maintenance] from their wealth.*"
> (Qur'an, 4:34)

Marriage is a partnership under the guidance and protection of Allah. For success in marriage, both partners need to work together as one unit to support each other. In this verse, the Qur'an explains that men are the head of the house, but that only happens when the man is fulfilling all of the rights of his spouse. Men need to be trying their best to provide for their partner, it's important to understand that men need to be fulfilling the rights of their spouse.

In this ever-changing world it is challenging to be able to find the balance, because in many relationships the woman could actually be earning more than her husband. That is okay, but the couple may need to discuss this and come to terms with it. Although it is the man's duty to pay for everything for his wife, it is acceptable if the wife wants to help pay towards the bills. Note it is not her right to do so, but in loving relationships this happens a great deal.

> "*They (your wives) are a clothing (covering) for you and you too are a clothing (covering) for them.*" (Qur'an, 2:187)

In our day-to-day life, we see many uses for clothing. Our clothes cover our body and protect them as well as beautifying us. The husband and wife are to play the same role in relation to one another. Your spouse is your support spiritually, emotionally, mentally and physically. When the relationship is working well the home becomes a place of protection and tranquillity, a paradise on earth, a place where one goes to restore their energy and prepare for another day in the dunya outside the home.

If the wife has spiritual defects or lacks something in her character, then the husband must cover these up and not expose her shortcomings to others. The wife too, must cover up and hide her husband's deficiencies and weaknesses and protect her mate. Not only has Allah (SWT) commanded the believers not to make fun of one another and not to mock or ridicule others, but they are also supposed to protect the honour and integrity of one another.

Sexual relations in marriage are a blessing. Islam teaches that having sexual relations with your spouse is an act of charity and you will be blessed for this action.

In the book 'Guidelines to Intimacy in Islam' by Mufti Muhammad ibn Adam Al-Kawthari, it explains that the enjoyment and fulfilment of sex in marriage is for the joy of both spouses. It states:

> "Islam protects the sexual rights of both the husband and wife, and to satisfy the sexual appetite of one's spouse is a

legitimate objective of sexual relations and even of marriage itself. The right of gratification belongs to both husband and wife, and it is a mistake to assume that only the husband has this privilege. The wife has as much right to expect her sensual needs to be fulfilled as the husband. As such, sensual gratification is the right of both spouses."

"*O you who believe! Do not forbid [for yourselves] the good things which Allah has permitted you; and do not exceed [the law] Allah does not like those who exceed [the law]. Therefore, eat of the lawful and good things that Allah has provided you, and fear Allah in whom you believe.*" (Qur'an, 5:87-8)

Marriage is recommended in Islam, and those that get married are seen as following the Sunna of Prophet Muhammad (ﷺ).

In this ayat just mentioned, Allah is stating to us, the Muslims, to not forbid something that He has given us. Allah is saying, do not forbid the good things – marriage is part of that.

I have a close friend that I grew up with and he didn't get married for a long while. He went on many dates with potential partners, but it never seemed to work for him. In the end he gave up and said to me, "I think I'm just meant to be on my own." This was a very sad state to be in.

But then I came across a sister who fitted his personality perfectly. When I spoke to him about the sister, he refused. But then my wife got involved and that made him sit up and give it a chance. He has been married for 15 years and has two beautiful children. Recently he said to me, "I cannot believe that I was wasting time outside of marriage; companionship is amazing, I wouldn't swap it for anything in the world."

In a famous hadith, the Prophet Muhammad (ﷺ) said that he loved three things: perfume, women and prayer and his heart was in the latter the most.

From this we can see that women and marriage were very close to the Prophet (ﷺ). He liked to see his community getting married.

The station of marriage in Islam is highly elevated. Marriage is the way of the Sunna and all those that follow the Sunna are following what Allah has said.

"Say (O Prophet): "If you really love Allah, then follow me, and Allah shall love you and forgive you your sins. Allah is Most-Forgiving, Very Merciful." (3:31)

To follow what the Prophet (ﷺ) did is highly recommended in Islam, and the best Muslims are those who are able to embody more of the practices of the Prophet of Islam.

So, as Muslims, it is clear that marriage is very important. It is something that brings humans closer to Allah. But this is not all marriages. This is only for the marriages that bring you close to Allah. The ones that do that are the ones where both parties have their rights, where love and respect are present and where the remembrance of Allah is also present.

If knowledge of Islam is present but love and compassion are not, that is a problematic gathering. In many marriages today, love and compassion are not present. Sometimes both couples are screaming for their rights, but no one is working on *rahma* (mercy) in the marriage.

The union of men and women is one of the most successful things that can happen in life. It helps both people to achieve the best in life – when they work together.

There is also the idea of having children; bringing them into the world. Prophet Muhammad (ﷺ) said:

> "*Each of you is a shepherd and each of you is responsible for his flock. The ruler is a shepherd and is responsible for his flock. A man is the shepherd of his family and is responsible for his flock. A woman is the shepherd of her husband's household and is responsible for her flock.*"

Marriage is a partnership. It's about two people coming together and becoming a team. In a relationship, each person has a different role to play. While it is the man's job to look after his wife, it is the woman's job to look after her family. Each should support the other.

While the roles they play in their relationship are different, they are both equal. There is equality in Islam; this is clear when you look at the teachings of the Qur'an. Allah says:

"For Muslim men and women, for believing men and women, for devout men and women, for true men and women, for men and women who are patient and constant, for men and women who humble themselves, for men and women who give in charity, for men and women who fast (and deny themselves), for men and women who guard their chastity, and for men and women who engage much in Allah's praise, for them has Allah prepared forgiveness and great reward." (Qur'an, 33:35)

Both of these roles are important for the smooth running of the relationship. In the relationship, the man has to lead by making decisions but only after consultation with his wife.

The Prophet Muhammad (ﷺ) on many occasions used to seek consultation from his wives when it came time to make difficult decisions. A great example is when, in the seerah, it talks about a time when the Muslims were on their way to make their first pilgrimage to Mecca.

They were very excited to make this pilgrimage but unfortunately when they got near to Mecca, they were stopped and told that they would not be allowed to enter Mecca that year to make their pilgrimage, but they would be allowed to make it next year. All of the Muslims at that time were very disappointed and upset that they were not being allowed to make the pilgrimage. The Prophet (ﷺ) realised that they would have to make their pilgrimage where they were, outside the city, so he told all of the companions to shave their heads, which is the act you do when you have completed the pilgrimage.

None of the companions responded as they were so sad and defeated because they wanted to have their head shaved in Mecca. When they did not listen, he (ﷺ) went to his wife and told her what had happened. She explained that they were all upset, but that they all loved and followed him. She advised him to go and shave his own head first and then all of the companions would follow.

That is exactly what happened.

Her name was Umm Salama, one of the wives of the Prophet (ﷺ). This is just one example of where the Prophet (ﷺ) sought counsel from one of his wives.

The role of a woman is to look after the children and bring them up well. It is also her job to be the first teacher of the children. That is why it is important that your wife is educated about the deen of Islam. When your wife is educated, then your children will also grow up educated about the deen.

Malcolm X famously quoted Dr. James Emmanuel Kwegyir-Aggrey:

> "When you teach a man you teach an individual, but when you teach a woman you teach a nation."

WHAT DOES THE SUNNA SAY ABOUT IT?

The Prophet (ﷺ) said:

> "If anyone likes to meet Allah in purity, then he should meet Him with a wife."

This hadith shows again the high station given to marriage in Islam. In today's society I meet many young professionals who are well established, but are dragging their feet towards getting married. This is the complete opposite to the times of the Prophet (ﷺ). The majority of the companions of the Prophet

(ﷺ) were married, and if they divorced they would soon be looking for a new partner.

> "*When one of you seeks a woman in marriage, and then if he is able to have a look at whom he wishes to marry, let him do so.*" (Dawood)

This hadith is very important and focuses on the idea of preference. It's important that you see the person that you want to marry and have a good look at them. Are you attracted to them? Do you like the look of them? Although beauty is not the be all and end all, it's important that you like the person that you are going to get married to. Beauty is not the only thing that should be looked upon but it's important to be attracted to the person you are hoping to spend the rest of your life with.

There are arranged marriages that happen where the groom doesn't see the bride until the marriage day. In some cases this works, but this is not following with what our dear Prophet (ﷺ) brought. You should look at your partner and make sure you find them attractive, as this is the person you plan to spend the rest of your life with.

It was narrated from Abdullah bin Amr that the Prophet (ﷺ) said:

> "*Do not marry women for their beauty, for it may lead to their doom. Do not marry them for their wealth, for it may lead them to fall into sin. Rather, marry them for their religion.*" (Ibn Majah)

When you marry for religion it doesn't mean that you don't marry for beauty, it means that religion is at the forefront. Of course you need to be attracted to your partner but that shouldn't be the main reason, as beauty will fade away with age. Sometimes, beauty can also be a mirage for a nice person. There are many physically beautiful people in this world who have the worst personalities.

There are many cases where people have made the mistake of marrying someone because they are beautiful or famous and have lived to regret it. Marrying just for wealth is also very dangerous because many people with wealth are extremely arrogant, this could lead to a very depressing existence especially if your partner is the one with the wealth and you don't have your own wealth.

Allah warns in the Qur'an in so many ayats about the danger of wealth (dunya). It is one of the largest distractions which leads people away from the path of Allah. Abu Hurairah (RA), narrated that the Prophet (ﷺ) said:

> "*A woman is married for four (reasons): her wealth, noble ancestry, beauty and religion. Choose the religious woman lest your hand is stuck to dust (because of destitution).*" (Bukhari & Muslim)

> "*Three groups of people Allah obliged Himself to help them: Mujahid in the cause of Allah, a worker to pay his debt, and the one who wants to marry to live a chaste life.*" (Tirmidhi)

The Prophet (ﷺ) said:

> "*One who marries has already guarded half of his religion, therefore he should fear Allah for the other half.*"

A person who can fulfil his sexual urges lawfully is less distracted in the spiritual journey. Love for women and faith are interrelated.

33

"When a man approaches his wife, he is guarded by two angels and [at that moment in Allah's view] he is like a warrior fighting for the cause of Allah. When he has intercourse with her, his sins drop like the leaves of the tree [in autumn season]. When he performs the major ablution, he is cleansed from sins." (Wasa'il ul-Shi'a, Vol. 14, p. 74)

It is narrated from Anas that Rasulallaah (ﷺ) said:

"Whosoever Allah has blessed with a righteous wife has been given half of his religion. He should fear Allah in the remaining half."

Sheikh Ibrahim Niasse (RTA) said in his Tafseer Fil Riyaadi Tafseer:

"Women are part of religion and that's why Rasool Allah (ﷺ) mentioned them in one hadith that: the only 3 things I'm allowed to love in your dunya are women, fragrance and salah".

Ibn Arabi said: "When a man loves a woman, he desires union, that is, the goal of union which exists in love. In the elemental form, there is no greater union than marriage."

There's a poem that says: "Women are fragrances of jannah (the garden of heaven) that Allah has created because of us and everyone of us is longing to perceive it..."

Some of the companions came to the wife of the Prophet (ﷺ) and asked her about his supplications. When they heard it they felt so little, to the extent that one of them said: "I will observe sawm (fast) till eternity and I will not break", another one said: "I will pray at night till eternity and I will not sleep" and another said: "I will distance myself from women till eternity and I will not marry". So when Rasool'Allah (ﷺ) heard them he said, "I am the best of you in knowing Allah and in fearing Him. I eat, I sleep and I have wives, that's my path and whosoever ignores my path is not from me."

Sheikh Ibrahim Niasse said in his Diiwan:

"Observe your daily salah, fast Ramadan, drink, eat, marry and join the family together, there's nothing there but the beauty of Mustapha Rasool'Allah (ﷺ)."

All of this shows that what Sheikh Ibrahim Niass (RTA) was explaining is that women are a blessing on this earth, and also that marriage is the way. It's also important that the lovers of Prophet Muhammad (ﷺ) get married as he loved marriage.

You learn a lot about yourself by being married and living with another individual. The world is more beautiful when you have a partner to experience it with. It can help you become a better person, as you have to learn how to relate with another human being.

WHEN IS A GOOD AGE TO GET MARRIED?

This is a good question: when is the best time to get married? To be honest with you, the best age depends on the individual. Some would say when you finish university and others would argue when you have finished your A levels. Others argue that the best age is when you have a good job and you are financially well off.

There is no right age to get married but there

should be some things in place. The person who wants to get married should be mature. The lowest age should be around 18 years. In some places, such as in the US, they would argue that it should be much higher – at 21.

The person should be working with access to their own money, secondly they should have a place to live. This doesn't necessarily mean their own place; it could be a room in their partner's family home, but this would need to be agreed by their partner.

Preparation

Marriage is a big step. It is one of the biggest decisions you will make in your life. Because of this, it is best to prepare for it before you take that final step.

In the Muslim community we are waking up to the importance of preparation, but we still have not reached the level where everyone is getting prepared before they get married.

Thousands of pounds are spent on the wedding day in every culture, but not even a fifth of that cost is spent on preparing the new couple for marriage.

In Islam, the idea of dating or having a steady boyfriend or girlfriend is frowned upon and because of this, in many cultures it does not happen. The main fear is that the couple may fall into illicit relations. Because of this, many newlyweds have no idea how to be in a relationship with another person. Many have no idea what happens after the wedding day. This is highly problematic because the most important part of the marriage is the marriage, which is actually living together day in day out.

Muslims need to be prepared for that part of married life which is the most important part. This includes knowing the rights of the man and woman in marriage. It also includes understanding about the sexual relationship in marriage. Sex is a very important part of a marriage and both partners should have an idea on how to please their partner. When this knowledge is acquired by both partners it will allow the marriage to develop smoothly and both partners will know what to expect and will not be shocked about what happens in the bedroom.

Another important action to do before marriage is to work on yourself. You can actually start to do this by speaking to the people who are close to you. They will be able to give you an idea on your character, on your flaws and what needs to be worked on.

If you have suffered from childhood traumas it's good to start to work on them before you get married. Many people don't do this then go into marriage with lots of destructive baggage. This may then go on to destroy the marriage.

In her book 'Before the Nikah', Dr. Nadir talks about the importance of doing that work before getting married. She cites a popular hadith from the Prophet Muhammad (ﷺ) that states:

> "*A man said 'O messenger of Allah, should I tie my camel and trust in Allah, or should I leave her untied and trust in Allah?' The Prophet said (ﷺ) 'Tie her and trust in Allah.'* (Sunan al-Tirmidihi 2517)

This hadith indicates the importance of doing work first, not just leaving everything to Allah without making any effort.

Marriage is a big step, so doing that inner work on yourself, working on your character, looking at any bad traits you have and working on them will go far in preparing you for marriage.

In a marriage blog called "Do Your Own Inner Work (The Secret to a Happy Marriage)," it spoke about 3 useful tools to help you on your journey of doing the inner work. These tools, if used correctly, will definitely benefit your relationship with your partner and will help to reduce conflict between you. The 3 tools are:

1. Practice mindfulness

2. Do the work

3. Create space

Practice Mindfulness

You've probably heard all about the science-backed benefits of mindfulness and meditation. You probably know that top performers in virtually every field rely on some form of mindfulness practice to ensure that they are not just physically fit but also mentally fit. To begin experiencing these benefits, set aside a small amount of time each day. Sit quietly with a straight spine and observe the sensations of each inhale and exhale. When your mind wanders, notice, and then gently bring your attention back to the sensations of each breath.

Mindfulness is key because it allows you to feel at peace with yourself. Once you are at peace with yourself you will then be able to benefit others around you including your partner. One of the dangers in relationships is bringing baggage from outside into your relationship. So for example, many people are dealing with stress, anger or other issues that have happened outside the home. If they are not checked before you are with your spouse, that can bring negative energy into your relationship. To deter this from happening, it is better if you spend some time relaxing your body and mind so that when you see your partner you don't pass on that negative energy.

Also, if you have experienced traumatic things in your day, share what has happened to you with your spouse; this will allow them to understand your behaviour if you feel a little bit tense.

We can also take an example from our beloved Prophet (ﷺ). Before Islam, the Prophet Muhammad (ﷺ) used to live in a problematic society that practiced many cultural things that the Prophet (ﷺ) did not like. These included burying their daughters alive, keeping slaves and worshipping idols.

The young Muhammad was upset with what he witnessed in his society, so to escape he would go to the cave to meditate. This was his way of practising mindfulness.

Do The Work

Another profound inner technology for expanding this gap between stimulus and response is a process for questioning your stressful thoughts called "Do The Work". It's a practice that pushes you to ask "is this true?" when experiencing the thoughts that trigger your stress, tension, and anxiety.

All of us experience negative thoughts, but it's important for us to reflect on them and ask the question, are these thoughts true? If they are not, you have to discard them and move on.

Patricia Harteneck, PhD, in an article on the website 'Psychology Today', talks about 7 ways to decrease negative thoughts. I found these really useful as it breaks down negative thoughts further and then gives beneficial advice on how to move past them.

Try these seven ways to manage (and decrease) your negative thoughts:

1. **Recognise thought distortions**. Our minds have clever and persistent ways of convincing us of something that isn't really true. These inaccurate thoughts reinforce

negative thinking. If you can recognise them, you can learn to challenge them. Here are four common thought distortions:

- Black and white thinking: Seeing everything as one way or another, without any in between.

- Personalising: Assuming you are to blame for anything that goes wrong, like thinking someone did not smile at you because you did something to upset her. (It's more likely that person is having a hard day and her mood had nothing to do with you.)

- Filter thinking: Choosing to see only the negative side of a situation.

- Catastrophizing: Assuming the worst possible outcome is going to happen.

2. **Challenge negative thoughts**. Whenever you have a distorted thought, stop and evaluate whether it is accurate. Think about how you would respond if a friend spoke about herself that way. You would probably

offer a good rebuttal to his or her negative view. Apply the same logic to your own thoughts. Ask yourself if you are assuming the worst will happen or blaming yourself for something that has not gone the way you wanted. And then think about other possible outcomes or reasons that something turned out differently than you hoped.

3. **Take a break from negative thoughts**. It is possible to learn how to separate from negative thoughts. One way to do this is to allow yourself a certain amount of time (maybe five minutes) with the thought, then take a break from focusing on it and move on with your day.

4. **Release judgement**. We all judge ourselves and others, usually unconsciously. Constantly comparing ourselves to other people or comparing our lives to some ideal breeds dissatisfaction. When you are able to let go of judgement (not easy, but possible), you will likely feel more at ease. Some ways

to take a break from judgmental thoughts include recognising your own reaction, observing it, and then letting it go. Another helpful technique is to "positive judge." When you notice you are negatively judging a person, yourself, or a situation, look for a positive quality, too.

5. **Practice gratitude**. Research shows that feeling grateful has a big impact on your levels of positivity and happiness. Even when you are experiencing a challenging time in your life, you can usually find things (even small things) to be grateful for. Noticing the things that are going well and making you feel happy will keep you in touch with them. Keeping a gratitude journal and writing a few things in it every day is one easy and effective way to do this.

6. **Focus on your strengths**. It's human nature to dwell on the negative and overlook the positive. The more you can practice focusing on your strengths and not dwelling

on mistakes you've made, the easier it will be to feel positive about yourself and the direction your life is taking. If you find yourself thinking harsh thoughts about your personality or actions, take a moment to stop and think about something you like about yourself.

7. **Seek out professional support** if you are unable to manage your thoughts or find they are interfering with your ability to meet your daily responsibilities or enjoy life. Counselling and therapy can help you weather life changes, reduce emotional suffering and experience self-growth.

Create Space

Many of us live in a state of constant doing. We're either working, caring for children, or stimulating our minds with social media, podcasts, Netflix bingeing, and the thousand or so other distractions of modern life.

Rarely, if ever, do we give ourselves and our mind space to simply be. Carving out space to intentionally break this habit is the final way to expand the space between stimulus and response.

Take a short stroll around the neighbourhood. Lie down on the couch for a brief power nap. Sit outside and gaze at the night sky. By giving yourself space, you're allowing your mind to breathe and enhancing your ability to navigate even the most contentious moments of marriage.

This is a brilliant piece of advice and so important to all of us living in big cities where it is always go! go! go! We need to create space for our mind so we can re-focus on what is important to us. Creating space could also be doing something you like. Going for a run, going for a coffee or going to the gym are also ways where you can give yourself space.

Life is so busy and sometimes we just need time to sit with ourselves and reflect on how we are doing and what is important.

Reading about marriage beforehand also helps. You may even go on a marriage course, so that you know what to expect when you are alone with your partner.

MONEY MATTERS

This is an important area to discuss before you get married. A high percentage of marriages end prematurely because the couple had different ideas about money: how to spend it, what to spend it on, what is important, and what is not important.

Spend time with your potential partner talking about your upbringing and how you grew up with money. Find out if your partner is a big spender or is frugal. If you are on different pages when it comes to money and how to spend it, this could lead to major issues in your relationship and ultimately could be what brings your relationship to an end.

In the teachings of Islam, it states that the husband's money is for taking care of his spouse and children if they come along. The wife's money is for herself, it is for her to do what she wills with it. If she wants to help you cover some of the bills she can but that is not her role, so she is not obliged to do that. It is the husband's role to fulfil this duty.

I find many men in today's society shunning marriage because of this reason.

I had a conversation with some young men in their late twenties, early thirties and they were expressing the view that marriage is expensive. They argued it's better to stay single so all of your wealth stays with you.

This is not a positive way to look at marriage, as to have a family and provide for them is the greatest act.

The foundation of Islam is the family, so if you are striving to do just that you are doing well by the teachings of Islam.

It's also very important for brothers to attain full time employment and have a secure place to live before they embark on the journey towards marriage. I hear stories of men who have no job and no secure place to live but are seeking to get married. So sisters make sure you thoroughly check the financial situation of your future spouse. Because if you are not careful, you might end up with a partner who is planning to live off of you.

The Four Agreements

'The Four Agreements' by Don Migel Riuz are ways of being which help you to be happier with yourself and be able to live a fulfilled life.

It's important that before you try to get into a serious relationship, you spend time working and developing yourself. The people who do this have a lot more to offer when they get married. This is because they have spent time working on themselves, so because of this they have less baggage.

The book takes inspiration from a set of spiritual beliefs held by the ancient Toltec people, to help readers transform their lives into a new experience of freedom, true happiness, and love.

According to the author, everything a person does is based on agreements they have made with themselves, with others, with God, and with life itself. In these agreements, people may tell themselves who they are, how to behave, what is possible, and what is impossible. Some agreements that individuals create may not cause issues, but there are certain agreements that come from a place of fear and have the power to deplete one's emotional energy as well as diminish the self-worth of a person. The book states that these self-limiting agreements are what creates needless suffering.

Ruiz also believes that to find personal joy, one must get rid of society-imposed and fear-based agreements that may subconsciously influence the behaviour and mindset of the individual. Another basic premise of the book suggests that much of suffering is self-created and that most of the time, individuals have the ability to transform themselves and the negative thoughts they may have about situations occurring within their life. The author identifies sources of unhappiness in life and proposes four beneficial agreements that one can make with oneself to improve one's overall state of well-being. By making a pact with these four key agreements, an individual is able to dramatically impact the amount of happiness they feel in their lives, regardless of external circumstances.

The Four Agreements are as follows:

Agreement 1: Be Impeccable With Your Word

Ruiz states that while this agreement is the most important, it is the most difficult one to honour. For this agreement, Ruiz first analyses the word 'impeccable'. The word impeccable comes from the Latin word *peccatus* meaning 'sin', and the *im* in the beginning of impeccable is the Latin prefix that means 'without'. Ruiz describes a sin to be anything that goes against oneself, and therefore being impeccable with language means to take responsibility for one's actions and remain without judgement against oneself and others. In essence, this agreement focuses on the significance of speaking with integrity and carefully choosing words before saying them aloud.

This is very important for successful marriages. You must try your best to live by your word, so that when you say you are going to do something, you try your utmost best to complete the task. If you are a person that lives by your word you will be respected by your partner and other people that know you. Many problems arise in marriage when partners don't keep their word. Every time another promise is broken another dark spot is on the heart of your partner until the heart becomes completely dark and at that moment that is when anything you say is not believed. This leads to lack of trust and when there is lack of trust in a relationship that is a clear sign that the union is crumbling.

The idea of choosing your words clearly is also very important. When you are a person who is able to choose your words wisely you are a person in good stead. This will allow you not to say things that you know will upset your partner. This will allow you to avoid many arguments by just being able to choose the right words. People who are not good at thinking before they speak are individuals that hurt their partner on many occasions with their words. Many times these individuals have no idea the damage their words can do to an individual. You usually find that those people who are not good at thinking before they speak are sometimes the same sort of people who can be guilty of emotional abuse, hurting their partner with their words.

The Prophet (ﷺ) was someone who was careful with his words. He only spoke when he needed to speak, on other occasions he was quiet. He (ﷺ) was also a good listener. Being a good listener is an important skill to have in a relationship.

Agreement 2: Don't Take Anything Personally

The second agreement provides readers with a way to deal with hurtful treatment from others that they may experience in life. It advocates the importance of having a strong sense of self and not needing to rely on the opinions of others in order to be content and satisfied with their self-image.

This agreement also allows readers to understand the notion that each individual has a unique worldview that alters their own perceptions, and that the actions and beliefs of a person is a projection of their own personal reality.

Ruiz believes that anger, jealousy, envy, and even sadness can lessen or dissipate once an individual stops taking things personally.

In Islam, it's important to put Allah first and then His Prophet Muhammad (ﷺ). A Muslim is a person who believes firmly in six foundations of imaan: in Allah, in angels, in the heavenly books, in the prophets and the messengers, in the day of judgement and in qadr (predestination). Among the bases of imaan, two are most important; one is faith in Allah, which is also called Tawhid, and the other is faith in His Messenger (ﷺ), which is called Risalat. It is expected that a true believer's life is always connected to Allah and His Messenger (ﷺ). He/she not only believes in Allah and His Messenger (ﷺ) by heart, but also wants to gain their pleasure to taste the sweetness of imaan. He/she loves Allah and His Messenger (ﷺ) and wants to gain their love. Almighty Allah says;

"*But those who believe and love Allah more (than anything else)*." (Qur'an, 2:165)

Those who put Allah and his Prophet (ﷺ) first are known as the believers. They do not only believe, but they put into action what they believe.

A believer loves Allah the most, performs ibadah (worship) for gaining the taste of His love and keeps away from evil deeds to escape His displeasure, as well as to gain reward from Him. Describing the characteristics of true believers, Allah, the Almighty says;

> "*Those who remain patient, seeking their Lord's countenance, establish salah, and spend out of that which I have bestowed on them, secretly and openly, and repel evil with good, for such, there is a good end.*" (Qur'an, 13:22).

Sometimes our friends, family and spouse can be a test for us. It's important to understand that and always remember that Allah is the most important. Don't rely on your spouse to be happy and fulfilled. You should be that already. Your spouse is a person that should help you on your journey to Allah. But sometimes your partner can be a test for you, that is why having patience is so important.

Before you get married you should be happy and confident in yourself and know your worth. So if you happen to be unfortunate to have a spouse that is treating you badly, don't take their hurtful words to heart, but be ready to challenge them on that. If they carry on being hurtful to you then seek guidance, talk to your parents, wali or any person you have on your side who is there to support you.

Agreement 3: Don't Make Assumptions

The third agreement describes the issue of making assumptions and how it leads to suffering, and why individuals should not partake in making them. When one assumes what others are thinking, it can create stress and interpersonal conflict because the person believes their assumption is a representation of the truth. Ruiz believes that a solution to overcoming the act of making an assumption is to ask questions and ensure that the communication is clear between the persons involved. Individuals can avoid misunderstandings, sadness, and drama by not making assumptions.

There is a saying of the Prophet Muhammad (ﷺ) where he explains that you should make excuses for your brother/sister if you hear something that doesn't sound right.

Al-Bayhaqi reported: Ja'far ibn Muhammad, may Allah have mercy on him, said, "If you hear something from your brother that you reject, make an excuse for him up to seventy excuses. If you cannot do it, then say: Perhaps he has an excuse I do not know."

It's important not to make assumptions but to go to the source and try to ascertain the truth. Many marriages fail because of hearsay. There are people around you that may not want the best for you and your family. Unfortunately, these types of individuals are happy to spread false rumours about you or a loved one.

When you have negative thoughts or ideas about your partner it is best that you find time to sit down and discuss what you have heard to get the truth. This will help to make sure that false rumours are not spread around.

Making assumptions can be very dangerous to your relationship, as it could mean you behaving in a negative way towards your partner. It could lead to stress, worry and anger, and it may be based on untruths.

During one of Prophet Muhammad's (ﷺ) journeys back to Medina from a battle, Aisha (RA) was present in the caravan. As the wife of Prophet Muhammad (ﷺ), she was given a special status and therefore, was covered during the travel in a small cabin with curtains, on a camel, to avoid heat and overexertion. During these journeys, the caravan would only stop once during the day and in this particular instance, they stopped during the night.

As they rested, Aisha (RA) left her cabin and went further into the desert to relieve herself. On her way back, she realised she had lost her necklace; one of special significance because it was given to her by the Prophet (ﷺ).

She became occupied with looking for her necklace, which was difficult because it was at night and in the desert. She was so occupied, she didn't realise the caravan was moving and the army didn't realise she wasn't in her cabin because the curtains were drawn and she was so lightweight there was no discernible difference. When Aisha (RA) finally found the necklace and realised she had been left behind, she laid down in the spot her camel had been and waited, hoping the caravan would return. Eventually, she fell asleep.

A Sahabah (companion of the Prophet (ﷺ) by the name of Sufwan (RA) was the man designated to travel further behind the caravan to ensure nothing was left behind. He discovered Aisha (RA) sleeping the next morning and upon identifying her, he backed up and said, "inna lillahi wa inna illayhi raji'un" (to Him we belong and to Him we return).

She woke up suddenly by his words – the only words that were ever spoken between them – and covered her face. He silently lowered the camel, she got on, and they travelled in complete silence back to Medina in broad daylight. A man by the name of Abdullah saw them return, and as someone who had a history of causing trouble among the believers, quickly set about insinuating things among the people in the city.

Upon her return home, Aisha (RA) fell extremely sick, enough for her to be unable to leave her house for an entire month. Meanwhile, rumours were spreading like wildfire about her, getting worse as they travelled from person to person and down the grapevine. When she was well enough to leave her home with her nurse at night, the rumours were revealed to her by her aunt. After hearing the news of these rumours being spread, Aisha (RA) asked to go back to her parents' home because she wanted to confirm what was being said by people she loved and couldn't bear for the words to leave the Prophet's (ﷺ) mouth. When it was confirmed by her parents, she fell even sicker and spent the entire night crying.

When Prophet Muhammad (ﷺ) spoke with Aisha (RA) about the situation, she decided that she wouldn't speak about it and put her complete faith in God. All she could say was what Yaqoub (AS) said to his sons – that she would have patience and belief that all would be okay by God.

While Aisha (RA) had complete faith in God and while she knew she was the wife of Prophet Muhammad (ﷺ), she was still so humble to think she wasn't important enough for ayats in the Qur'an to be revealed about her.

The ayats that were revealed are, even to this day, powerful in their message and guidance.

Verses revealed in Surah An-Noor (24:11-21), revealed not only Aisha's (RA) innocence, but also came as the clarification of what is wrong with slander and accusations as well as the necessity of evidence and witnesses. These ayats are the foundation of justice for how we treat one another in mankind. These ayats go to prove that starting rumours and accusations about one another is incredibly harmful and wrong, but that in the face of accusations being spread to you or about you, the best option is to stop speaking entirely and remove yourself from the situation.

Our belief in God and Islam depends on how we treat and talk about Muslims and if there is no evidence, the accused must be believed as completely innocent. Even if something seems true or easily proven to be, we must understand that God is the only judge that matters. We should put ourselves in the situation of those who are the subject of the rumours that are spread.

What we can learn about the Prophet's (ﷺ) reaction to the situation is that he went to talk with Aisha about the rumours that were being shared, he didn't hide it from her. In this case the Qur'an was revealed to inform everyone that she was innocent, but in today's society if you find yourself in this position it's best to talk to the person involved. When you don't do that, resentment and anger could be building up in your body and may manifest in a harmful way for all involved.

When you have bad thoughts about something your partner said it's best for you to find time to talk to your partner about it. When you do that you have a chance to get clarity about what was said and this can clear up any misconceptions. When you don't do that you add two and two and come up with seven. Miscommunication is a great cause for problems in a relationship, so it's best to try to make sure you understand your partner as much as possible.

Agreement 4: Always Do Your Best

The fourth agreement allows readers to have better insight into achieving progress towards their goals in life. This agreement entails integrating the first three agreements into daily life and also living to one's full potential. It involves doing the best that one can individually manage, which varies from the different situations and circumstances that the individual may encounter. Ruiz believes that if one does their best in any given moment, they will be able to avoid self-judgement and regret. By incorporating the first three agreements and doing the best they can in all facets of life, individuals will be able to live a life free from sorrow and self-ridicule.

In Islam, we have the teaching that we should

strive for excellence in all areas. So whatever we are working on, we should put our full focus on it and try our best to reach excellence (Ihsan) in all of our actions.

So for example, when we are learning knowledge, we should try our best to be excellent at that. We have examples of the pious predecessors that travelled long distances just to collect one saying of the Prophet Muhammad (ﷺ). The reason why they did this is because of the respect they have for knowledge.

In your relationship, always try your best to make sure your partner is happy and you are doing your bit to make sure the relationship is going well. The best relationships are those that the couple spend time on. To have a successful union takes time and effort. Those that don't spend time developing their bond are making their relationship vulnerable to problems.

Communication Is Key

One of the most important ingredients of a successful marriage is communication. Communication is the bedrock where everything else can be built on top of. Communication allows the couple to know how they are feeling about their relationship. When there is good communication in a relationship, you find good and rich connections. Strong bonds are built with good communication. This only works when both parties are actively communicating, it doesn't work if one side is not telling the other person how they are feeling.

Steve Keller in his book 'Communications and Relationships', stresses the importance of working at making sure that the relationship is good, comes from both sides and is constant.

He states there are 3 reasons for marriages to break up:

1. Wrong assumptions

2. Confusions

3. Misunderstandings

He explains that good communication can help to alleviate these issues in a relationship. He states, "communication is the best way to resolve marital conflicts."

Steve Keller also explains that mutual respect is very important for a strong relationship. Respect has to come from both sides; both individuals need to actively show love and respect to each other. In relationships disagreements will arise, but when there is respect in a relationship then problems can be sorted out in a respectful manner. Always try to discuss disagreements in a calm and respectful way.

It's also very important to understand that no one is perfect. The only perfect person was the Prophet Muhammad (ﷺ), the rest of us are imperfect. Nobody can change themselves completely, but with effort there are many things that we can change about ourselves if we try hard enough.

It's also important that both sides of the marriage need to be accountable for telling their partner what they are doing wrong. But this should be done in a nice and respectable way. When it is done in a rude way, it doesn't support positive outcomes.

Misunderstandings can happen very easily in a marriage especially when there is poor communication. A person can read into a situation wrongly without having a conversation about the issue. A friend once said to me; there are always three opinions in any situation: his version, her version and the truth. I thought this was brilliant because we all have our own opinion on any situation, but our thoughts may not lead to the true picture of what really happened. Our mind is constantly interpreting every experience we have.

Stehen Covey, in his ground-breaking book 'The 7 Habits of Highly Effective People', discusses the idea of empathic communication. He discusses the importance of understanding where the other person is coming from before you react. Too many times we find ourselves in situations where there is a disagreement but we don't understand where the other person is coming from.

Being an empathic communicator means you have listened carefully and have truly tried your utmost best to understand where the other person is coming from. Listening actively to a partner's point of view and then showing them sincerely that you hear them and understand can really help. When you do this effectively and then have been able to let the other person know that you understand their point of view, this puts the other person at ease and allows them to be more open to your response. This is because they believe that you truly understand their point of view.

EMOTIONAL BANK ACCOUNT

This is an idea coined by Stephen Covey in "The 7 Habits of Highly Effective People." He talks about the idea of an 'emotional bank account' which we fill up by doing good actions, by showing understanding, kindness and respect, keeping promises and by having integrity. All of these actions help to increase your emotional bank account.

What empties out the bank account is negative actions. Covey calls these withdrawals. An example of these are things like showing unkindness, discourtesy and disrespect, also by breaking promises, being disloyal and holding grudges. All of these are examples of a lack of integrity. All of these actions will empty out your emotional bank account. Once your bank account is empty and goes into overdraft, this indicates that your relationship is in real danger.

You could be heading towards a break up or divorce if you are married. Marriage is a situation which takes a lot of work, those who don't work on it are heading towards a break up.

The Prophet Muhammad (ﷺ) stated that marriage is half of your deen, but the other part of it is extensive work to make sure that it lasts and that it is meaningful and valuable for your partner.

The idea of the emotional bank account is a great metaphor. It helps you to have the understanding that you have to work on yourself and your relationship for it to be successful.

FORGIVENESS

Forgiveness is one of the main elements that needs to be in a relationship. The reason for this is that none of us are perfect, we always make mistakes. Some of these shortcomings happen when we upset other people and when we do that we would love for them to forgive us.

Allah has said in the Qur'an about forgiveness towards fellow beings; no matter how much they have hurt you, "...They should rather pardon and overlook. Would you not love Allah to forgive you? Allah is Ever-Forgiving, Most Merciful." (Qur'an, 24:22)

In relationships, forgiveness is key; this is the place where you gain your most love and support. It's paramount that you try your level best to make sure that your marriage is rock solid. One of the elements that makes sure that it is rock solid is forgiveness. When this is present in a marriage it gives it a chance to grow and flourish. In every relationship there will be trials and tribulations but when forgiveness is a key element, it makes all the challenges easier to get through. Abu Hurairah (May Allah be pleased with him) said:

> "*The Messenger of Allah (ﷺ) said: 'By the One in Whose Hand my soul is! If you did not commit sins, Allah would replace you with a people who would commit sins and seek forgiveness from Allah; and Allah will certainly forgive them.'*"

Asking Allah for forgiveness is seen by all scholars as a praiseworthy action. The Prophet Muhammad (ﷺ) used to ask for forgiveness 70 to 100 times a day. The reason he did this was not for himself, because Allah had already forgiven any shortcomings he made. This was done to teach us, the followers of the Prophet (ﷺ), how to ask for forgiveness and how regularly we should be doing it.

It is also clear that as Muslims we should seek forgiveness from the creation of Allah when we wrong them. This is seen as a good practice.

In a Hadith (Muslim), Abu Umamah reported:

> "*The Messenger of Allah, peace and blessings be upon him, said: 'I guarantee a house on the outskirts of Paradise for one who leaves arguments even if*

75

he is right, and a house in the middle of Paradise for one who abandons lies even when joking, and a house in the highest part of Paradise for one who makes his character excellent."' (Sunan Abī Dāwūd)

Here again in this hadith we see the excellence of forgiveness where it is stated that the one who leaves arguments even when they are right. This is seen as a noble action and it will lead to a more peaceful atmosphere. The one who is always ready to argue will suffer from having a home which is not filled with peace and harmony.

THE FIVE APOLOGY LANGUAGES

Author and counsellor Gary Chapman created the five apology languages. These five give you a more in depth look at the different types of apologies.

The five are:

1. Expressing regret

2. Accepting responsibility

3. Making restitution

4. Genuinely repenting

5. Requesting forgiveness

Many people have one kind of apology language but here is an overview of them all.

1. Expressing regret is the art of verbally saying "I am sorry." Even though this seems very easy, there are many people who find this very difficult. Usually these are people with big egos, they are the types that think they are always right.

2. Accepting responsibility is being able to apologise but to also be clear on what you are sorry for, indicating what you have done wrong. This is a more sincere apology. There are many people who apologise but don't understand why they are saying it. They say the words to get peace, but they have not understood what they have done wrong. This is highly problematic because the person could then easily go and do the same thing again because they have not understood what they have done wrong in the first place.

3. Making restitution is where the person tries to find a way to fix the situation. This can happen if something is lost or broken.

4. Genuinely repenting comes with a change of behaviour. This is very good, as the person has understood what they have done wrong and have taken steps to change their problematic behaviour.

5. Requesting forgiveness allows the other person time to reflect on the apology and to see if they accept it. This type of apology is sincere because the person wants to make sure that the hurt party has accepted their apology and if their relationship has been repaired.

THE WIPE OUT

The wipe out is a technique that can also be used to fix issues in relationships. We are all humans, so we say and do things out of anger. We say things that we wish we could take back, but we know that we can't because the other person has heard it and has already been affected by it. The wipe out works by asking our partner for a wipe out when we have said something really bad out of anger or frustration which we wish we never said.

If your partner agrees to give you a wipe out, that means that they forgive you and what you said has been erased from their memory and cannot be brought up again. This is a great way to reset difficult situations we get into, as we are not perfect. We all say and do things that we regret later. So this wipe out technique is a brilliant way to reset and prepare for a bad circumstance.

Cross-Cultural Marriage

Cross-cultural marriage in Islam is still a taboo in many communities. Even in the UK, where there are more and more cross-cultural marriages happening, they are still met with problematic perceptions.

There are many reasons why this is the case. One of the biggest reasons is because of tribalism, racism and colourism. Some cultures do not want their children to get married to someone of a different tribe let alone a different race. I have worked with many clients where the woman wants to get married to her partner who happens to be black from Africa or the Caribbean and the family refuses based on racism.

This is problematic as Islam is not racist; it is perfect, but some of the Muslims still hold racist and negative views about other Muslims. When clients have come to me and explained the situation, I have always advised them that it is better to take things slow and try to get the family with prejudiced views to change their mind. On many occasions this has helped to bring the family around.

But I also explain to couples that if the racism or prejudice is deep rooted in the family, it may be better off to call it quits because if they go forward and get married this will cause a lot of heartache later on in the marriage.

> "Clarity regarding individual and family views on cross cultural marriage and interfaith marriage before you marry is a key before the Nikah principle". (Nadir, 2021)

It is very important to understand how your parents feel about cross-cultural marriage. We know in the teachings of Islam that cross-cultural marriages are recommended, but in reality it is a totally different experience.

Allah states in the Qur'an:

"O mankind! We created you from a single (pair) of a male and a female, and made you into nations and tribes, that ye may know each other (not that ye may despise (each other). Verily the most honoured of you in the sight of Allah is (he who is) the most righteous of you. And Allah has full knowledge and is well acquainted (with all things)." (49:13)

Allah states clearly that He created different tribes and nations so that we could get to know each other, learn about each other's different cultures and celebrate the diversity we have inside Islam.

This being said, ignorance, racism and a lack of tolerance for difference is alive and well inside many Islamic communities. Because of this, marrying someone from outside your culture can cause major upheavals in the family. It is best to be aware of what kind of family you have before you start to plan to marry someone.

This doesn't mean it can never happen. I have many friends and associates who are happily married in mixed relationships, but for many of them they had to go through many trials before they got to the stage to enjoy marital bliss.

In some cases, it is possible to win your parents around but in other cases it is not possible. Although this is wrong, it is a reality in many Muslim families and if your family is like that, it may be better for you to marry in your culture so that you won't have to go through family problems.

Dawud Walid in an article entitled 'Interracial' Marriage in the Prophetic Era', discusses the issue of interracial marriage. He starts off by explaining that it is not a bad thing to favour your own culture for marriage, but it becomes a problem when you try to block people from getting married because of the ethnicity of one of the couple. He writes:

> "There is nothing wrong with Muslims looking for mates firstly within their own ethnic groups. Having preferences in and of themselves also do not make those holding them to be racists, though standards of beauty or suitability can be implicitly biased, shaped by broader historical and societal factors."

Parents having such preferences in and of themselves are also not clear signs of ethnic bigotry. The Prophet (ﷺ) stated: "A woman can be married for four [reasons]: Her wealth, her family status, her beauty and her deen, so select deen [as most important] that you may be blessed."

An-Nawawi stated in his commentary on this tradition that the Prophet (ﷺ) was speaking to the people based upon the customs of what they looked for relating to marriage. Based upon these, it is not blameworthy to be inclined to marry someone firstly within one's culture, or for parents to have that desire for their children to seek to marry based upon families known to them, which usually has some sort of village or ethnic connection. The problem comes when deen is relegated to culture, or if people hold animosity or try to block others from getting married simply because of ethnic or cultural differences. Thankfully, the Prophetic tradition sheds light on this subject for us.

Walid goes on to explain that in the Prophetic era, the Prophet (ﷺ) was busy marrying people together who came from different cultures. For him (ﷺ), the most important thing was character. He explains:

Regarding the Sahabah, there were several of them who were in inter-tribal or inter-ethnic marriages. Moreover, some of these marriages were specifically arranged by the Prophet (ﷺ). In mentioning the permissibility of such marriages, Imam Zayd bin Ali bin al-Husayn bin Ali bin Abi Talib (may Allah's blessings be upon them) made note of some of the Sahabah who were in such unions:

Zayd bin Harithah, a former slave from the Kalb tribe, married Zaynab bint Jahsh, a lady from Quraysh. Bilal married Halah bint 'Awf, the sister of Abdur Rahman bin 'Awf [who was the richest of the Sahabah]. Zurayq, a man freed from slavery by the Messenger of Allah, married 'Amrah bint Bishr bin Abi 'Al-Aws bin Umayyah. Abdullah bin Razah, a man freed from slavery by Mu'awiyah, married bint 'Amr bin Hurayth. Ammar bin Yassir married the sister of 'Amr bin Hurayth. Abu

Mijdham bin Abi Fakihah married a lady from Bani Zuhrah.

Besides the Prophet (ﷺ) arranging Zayd bin Harithah's marriages to Zaynab bint Jahsh and later to Barakah al-Habashiyyah (may Allah be pleased with them), some of the other inter-tribal marriages arranged by him include:

- Al-Miqdad bin 'Amr to Duba'a bint az-Zubayr, the daughter of the Prophet's (ﷺ) paternal uncle

- Usamah bin Zayd to Fatimah bint Qays al-Qurashiyyah

- Sa'ad al-Aswad to bint 'Amr bin Wahb

- Julaybib to a lady from the Ansar

The Prophet (ﷺ) knew the qualities of the men which he sought out marriage for on their behalf. In the process of doing so, he was taking a step in dismantling the tribal chauvinism of the Hijazi Arabs as it relates to whom their children could marry. He encouraged parents to deprioritize tribal affiliation and social class in favour of spiritual virtue. Thus, the Prophet (ﷺ) instructed, "If someone comes to marry and you are pleased with his deen and his character, then marry him. If not, there will be chaos and widespread corruption on the earth."

What Does Society Say About Love And Marriage?

Society gives out mixed messages when it comes to love. This is because society is hyper-sexualised. All of the films and programs we all watch on TV always have a large focus on relationships, especially sexual relationships. There are many problems with the messages that they are giving out. For example, they advocate to have sex whenever you feel ready and you are at the age when it is allowed by law, which is 16 in the UK.

This kind of advice flies in the face of our belief as Muslims. We follow the holy Qur'an and the Sunna of Prophet Muhammad (ﷺ). We are taught that sex is good and is a blessing when it is done right, and according to Islam that is when it takes place inside marriage; which is a union blessed by Allah.

Muslims face many challenges today; it is extremely challenging to do the right thing and follow what Allah says in the Qur'an and Sunna when everyone around you is not doing that and is going with the status quo.

Today we find many Muslims that are involved in haram relationships, having sexual relationships outside of marriage. This is very unfortunate but is a challenge of our time. Muslims are becoming more and more secularised following the culture of the people around them. This has led to lots of problems for young Muslims.

The way around this is to first gain more knowledge of the deen of Islam and surround yourself with believers, those who learn about the deen (religion) and practice it. It is possible to have friends that are not Muslim, but what is really important is if they respect your culture and give you space to follow what your religion tells you. If your friends are good and understanding they can even help you; when they see you coming close to forbidden acts they can warn you to be careful and even shield you from it.

It's very important to understand that once you

have lost your innocence you can't get it back. But if you do find yourself in this predicament, as many young Muslims find themselves today, it's not the end of the world.

The Qur'an declares:

> "*Say: 'O my Servants who have transgressed against their souls! Despair not of the Mercy of Allah: for Allah forgives all sins: for He is Oft-Forgiving, Most Merciful.'*" (39:53)

The verse explains that it is never too late to move forward. Part of moving forward is making sincere repentance that you will not do the act again and working towards living a righteous life.

I know that these steps are not easy, that's why it is important to take one step at a time. It's important to understand that everything that Allah wants us to do is for the best.

> "*Allah intends for you ease and does not intend for you hardship.*" (Qur'an, 2:185)

Marriage is part of the idea of creating peace for the individual. When two people find themselves in a loving relationship, this makes travelling the path of life much easier. Life is filled with many trials and tribulations, but having a loving and supporting partner is the best thing in the world.

In Surat Al-Ma'idah, verse 6, Allah (SWT) says:

> "...*Allah does not intend to make difficulty for you...*"

In Surat Al-A'raf (7:157), we read that the Prophet (ﷺ) has been sent so that he commands people to good and he forbids them what is evil.

Marriage is seen as a great good in Islam. It is a blessed action which pleases Allah and also the beloved Prophet (ﷺ). It will also act as a protection against committing evil acts, for example sexual activity outside of marriage.

PREPARING THE MAN

According to the teachings of Islam, the man is the head of the household. He should provide for his wife financially, make sure she is clothed and fed and has a place to stay. In these ever-changing times this can sometimes be very challenging. The way to deal with this is through communication. Sometimes the wife may be the breadwinner or making more money than her husband. This is not something to be ashamed of, but this can happen a great deal as women are becoming highly educated and are getting rewarded for their talents.

In this situation it may cause different dynamics in the relationship. The best way to move forward successfully is to discuss the situation with your wife and what you can provide. According to the teachings of Islam, the man should provide for his wife and his money is her money and her money is her own. But when the relationship is good this can be negotiated where both partners can share the bills.

Before marriage the man should work on himself. If he has any conditions where he needs to see a counsellor, that should be done before marriage. This is very important so that he will be able to go into the marriage with positive characteristics that he will be able to share with his wife.

Many times, men go into a marriage without doing work on themselves. This is very dangerous. It can lead to severe problems in the marriage, including emotional or physical abuse. For example, if a man has anger issues, he should seek counselling before the marriage. If not, this could lead to him abusing his wife. I have witnessed this where a brother married a sister but he had anger issues which came out in the marriage and this led to him physically abusing his wife. This situation could have been prevented if the man had gone to see a counsellor before he got married, allowing him a safe space and time to work on himself before marriage. This is also possible in reverse where a woman is physically abusive towards the man.

Sometimes parents are guilty of this; they let their son marry someone when they know there are many problems that their son has, such as drinking alcohol, gambling or unresolved anger issues.

It is also important for a man to know about his strengths and weaknesses before going into a marriage. This will definitely help him prepare for marriage. It's very important to understand that everyone can change. In Islam we are taught that it takes 40 days to create a habit. This means that you can create a way of being and stick to it. This also means you can change a bad habit into a positive habit. The most important thing to understand is that all of this takes time and work.

Once, the Prophet (ﷺ) explained that if a person spent time working on themselves they would have no time to focus on others, as to focus on oneself is a full-time job. This hadith clearly points out that to work on yourself becoming a better human being is no small feat.

It is a large job that will take all of your life, because you will always be refining your character as no one person is perfect. That station is only for the Prophets (AS).

Preparing the Woman

Marriage is about partnership; about being there for one another. No one is perfect so it is about supporting each other. When both parties are working together, supporting each other in every way, then it becomes a place of bliss and blessings.

Preparation for marriage is important for both men and women, where they need to work on themselves.

If a person has gone through traumatic

experiences in their life, it's important to get professional help from a counsellor.

Part of the preparation of marriage is getting to know your intended partner, knowing their hopes and dreams. These should be things that you agree with; when this happens you can work together as a team to work towards them. It's also important for your partner to know about your hopes and dreams for the same reason. One of the reasons why marriages crumble is when the hopes and dreams of the individuals are not expressed, or the other person has no idea about what the other person wants.

One of the most sacred acts between a married couple is love making. In Islam this is something that, when it is done right, in a loving relationship, is an act of worship. It's important to know how to please your partner and what your partner likes. It's also important to learn about how to be sexual and alluring to make the activity beautiful and fulfilling. Remember, according to the teachings of Islam, love making is a good action, where you will be rewarded for when it is done right.

Na'ima B. Roberts in her book, 'Show Up', advises Muslim women about relationships. She writes:

"What does it mean to 'show up' as a spouse?

Again, the call to being present and mindful, to being sincere and authentic and bringing your true self to the relationship. This can be difficult for some of us, particularly if we have been taught there is only one way to be a good wife OR if we have been hurt before. In either scenario, it is often easier to simply play the role of the good wife, to do the duties, to say the right things and protect ourselves from being vulnerable and, potentially, getting hurt. This way, we are safe from judgement and criticism.

But are we truly loving and supporting from an authentic place, as our true selves? Do we dare to do that?

"Your wives are a garment for you, and you are a garment for them." (Qur'an, 2:187)

Often, when this verse is mentioned,

we are reminded that garments protect and beautify, making us feel loved, secure and safe. Showing up as a wife means doing all this from a place of sincerity and authenticity, from a place of contentment and gratitude.

When we show up as wives who are garments, we strive to adapt, to change. To grow to accommodate our spouse as he grows, or to come in a little, when he needs a little extra support."

EMOTIONAL INTELLIGENCE

Emotional intelligence is the ability to understand, use, and manage your own emotions in positive ways to relieve stress, communicate effectively, empathise with others, overcome challenges and defuse conflict. Emotional intelligence helps you build stronger relationships, succeed at school and work, and achieve your career and personal goals. It can also help you to connect with your feelings, turn intention into action, and make informed decisions about what matters most to you.

In an article written by Hosai Mojaddidi entitled, 'Emotional Intelligence Personified: How Following the Sunnah Can Save Your Marriage', she writes about the importance of knowing about yourself and explains:

> Ibn Arabi said, "He who knows himself, knows his Lord." In other words, self-knowledge precedes knowledge of God. Thus, our young boys and girls need to learn basic lessons on personality differences, temperaments, and gender differences from an Islamic framework. These subjects provide a critical context to help shape the way young people perceive the world around them and understand their faith, thus they will prove useful for the study of important core subjects such as fiqh, hadith, seerah, and Qur'an.

> Emotional intelligence gives you a better understanding of yourself and when you have this you will gain a deeper understanding of your creator,

the one who created you. When you are someone on the path of tazkiyaat an-nafs (purification of the soul) this means you are on the path of becoming a better person. You wish to rid yourselves of deadly characteristics like greed, anger, jealousy, envy, hatred and selfishness. This knowledge will also benefit you in your relationship with your partner.

Furthermore, as our tradition teaches us, the lifelong struggle for every Muslim is the rigorous pursuit of self-development or tazkiyaat an-nafs (purification of the soul). By teaching young men and women to look inward and to understand themselves on a deeper level we will help to facilitate this deeply intense spiritual process. Additionally, the skills and knowledge they acquire will help them in their future relationships once they are ready to marry.

Mojaddidi also explains why having a deeper knowledge of the workings of the emotions of a person can help to make you a better partner. She explains:

> A man, for example, who understands well the differences in male and female patterns of behaviour, communication styles, and brain structure, and is fully aware of the impact of a woman's physiology on her physical form, her emotional state, and her overall disposition, is far better equipped to deal with the natural changes his wife may endure throughout their marriage.

> Conversely, men who are unaware of or have very limited and superficial knowledge of these things may not know how to interpret the differences in mood, behaviour, and physical changes in their wives, and may even become apathetic, resentful, or abusive towards them.

This is why studying and learning about emotional intelligence is essential knowledge for any person who is planning to go into a relationship with another human being.

Emotional intelligence is commonly defined by four attributes:

1. Self-management – You're able to control impulsive feelings and behaviours, manage your emotions in healthy ways, take initiative, follow through on commitments, and adapt to changing circumstances.

2. Self-awareness – You recognise your own emotions and how they affect your thoughts and behaviour. You know your strengths and weaknesses, and have self-confidence.

3. Social awareness – You have empathy. You can understand the emotions, needs, and concerns of other people, pick up on emotional cues, feel comfortable socially, and recognise the power dynamics in a group or organisation.

4. Relationship management – You know how to develop and maintain good

relationships, communicate clearly, inspire and influence others, work well in a team, and manage conflict.

In self-management you are able to control yourself. In Islam this is the idea of controlling your ego. Sheikh Ibrahim Niass, a great religious leader, once said, "who rides who?" He was referring to the ego and what he meant by that is; check yourself. It's important as Muslims that we should be in control of our ego. When that is not the case it can lead to major problems in your life, e.g. Illicit affairs, sex outside of marriage and breaking all of the laws that Allah has put in the Qur'an and Sunna of the Prophet (ﷺ).

Praying five times a day and fasting in Ramadan are two of the pillars that focus on training the ego and instilling discipline into the body. The Islamic science of tassawuf is that which focuses on disciplining the ego. Imam Ghazali, a great Muslim scholar from the 10th century, has written a lot about the idea of controlling the ego. It is true that those that control their ego will have more success and be able to live a more disciplined life than those who don't know how to control themselves.

Self-awareness is the idea of knowing yourself. You are aware of your strengths and weaknesses. The second caliph of Islam, Umar al Khattab, was someone who had good self-awareness. He was constantly looking over himself and checking his actions and intentions. Every night he would sit down and reflect on his day, he would think of all the good he did and would praise Allah. He would also look at all of the bad he did then ask Allah for forgiveness. We don't have to go to that length that Umar (RA) went to, but this is a good example of a person who is checking himself, making sure he can be the best he can.

Those who don't watch over themselves are in danger of corrupting themselves. It's important to understand that no-one is perfect, the only one who was perfect was the Prophet Muhammad (ﷺ) that is why Allah said about him:

> "*And indeed, you are upon a noble conduct, an exemplary manner.*" (Qur'an, 68:4)

The Prophet (ﷺ) was the epitome of graciousness, courtesy and good breeding. His character, manners and behaviour were worthy of emulation.

Malik reported: The Messenger of Allah, peace and blessings be upon him said:

"I have been sent to perfect good character." (al-Muwatta' 1614)

Sex in Marriage

Sex in Islam is a very important part of marriage and unfortunately it has been the part that has been the most neglected. This is very wrong because every topic in Islam should be spoken about without shyness or shame. Sex in Islam is seen as a blessing, but it is also seen as something that both partners should really enjoy.

There is a big myth surrounding sex in Islam. This is because when non-muslims see our women walking around covered up they think that Muslims don't enjoy sexual relations, but this is very wrong.

One evidence of this is the amount of Muslim children you see prevalent in any Muslim community. This is evidence that sexual relations are happening regularly. It's also important to understand that sex is not just seen as a way of bringing new life into the world, it is also a way for a couple to express their love and affection for each other.

It's very important for both men and women to gain knowledge of what should be happening in the bedroom. We should not get our knowledge about this from watching pornography as this does not give a true picture of what intimacy is.

In the book 'The Muslimah Sex Manual' by Umm Muladat, she breaks down the false myth that Muslims don't have a lot of sex. She writes:

"I don't know who started this myth but it is flat wrong. We have halal and we have haram. Any sexual encounter outside of marriage is haram. Everything inside marriage is halal (other than a tiny number of things which I will mention in the book). You can be pure as snow and still be very dirty in the bedroom. What is amusing in a sad way is that many younger Muslims think that the practising, masjid going, hijab/niqab wearing sisters have dull sex lives and never venture outside of the vanilla. Not true! I have a theory that Muslims are actually kinkier than non-Muslims because we bottle up all that sexual energy and provide only one outlet, that of marriage. Whatever the reason though, I can assure you that some of the same Muslim men and women giving halaqahs and khutbas and volunteering at the masjid are having very raunchy sex behind closed doors."

Dr. Aneesah Nadir explains about the importance of knowledge of sexual relationships:

"Problems related to an unsatisfactory or absent physical relationship tend to occur because no one has spoken with the young man or woman about these matters prior to marriage. Often, the prospective couple is unaware about the physical makeup of the human body or is unaware of the Islamic responsibility and right to intimate fulfilment by both parties. Inability to communicate seems to exacerbate the problem unless professional intervention is obtained."

Marriage preparation education will educate potential spouses of their rights and responsibilities with regard to sexual fulfilment. It would also provide an opportunity to learn some basics of the human anatomy as well as the traditions of Prophet Muhammad (ﷺ) with regard to marital intimacy. The role of good communication skills in sexual fulfilment would also be a part of premarital education.

THE BENEFITS OF SEX IN MARRIAGE

Sex in Islam is seen as a highly beneficial activity. It is an action that is highly rewarded by Allah (SWT), so when a couple is engaged in sexual activity they are gaining rewards for their actions. Scholar Habeeb Akande discusses the benefits of sexual relations in his book, "A taste of honey".

He explains:

"A tradition related by many erotologists states "When a husband and his wife look at each other lovingly, Allah will look at them with his merciful eye. When they hold hands their sins will fall away from between their fingers. When they engage in coitus they will be surrounded by prayerful angels. For every sensation of their delight there is a counterpart of reward for them in the garden as huge as a mountain. If the wife conceives, she will have a reward of a worshipper who is constantly engaged in prayer, fasting and in the struggle, in the way of Allah. When she delivers a child only Allah knows the magnitude of the rewards stored for the parents in the garden."

From this quote you can see that just looking at your partner in a loving way is a beneficial action, as well as just holding hands. In this quote he also explains that the benefit of sexual relations is not something that is rewarded in this life, but it is something that will be rewarded in the hereafter.

What I found so interesting about this quote is the idea that even being pregnant is a blessed state to be in which is rewarded by Allah. And the act of giving birth and bringing another human into this world is rewarded by Allah and is also given a high regard.

This makes even more sense when you think of the famous hadith of the Prophet (ﷺ), where he states that 'heaven is at the foot of the mother'.

Habeeb carries on to quote a psychologist who discusses the psychological benefit of sex in marriage.

He writes:

> "Professor of sociology and author of sexuality in Islam, Abdulwahab Bouhdiba said "sexual intercourse applied in the laudable way has many beneficial effects. It drives away grieving, subdues melancholic depression, epilepsy and irascibility, it reduces corpulence resulting from the retention of the phlegmatic moistures, diminishes the frequency of nightly pollutions, improves digestion, stimulates the appetite and prevents a disease called paralysis of

the soul (butlan an-nafs) entailing the occurrence of fainting fits. This is not only valid for men but also for women, because their bodies function in a way parallel to the bodies of men and equally produce sperm which is emitted during sexual activity, an idea taken over from ancient medical theory."

So it's clear to see that sexual intercourse is a very important part of a marriage, and it benefits the couple spiritually, physically and psychologically.

THE IMPORTANCE OF FOREPLAY

Foreplay is very important for couples that want to have deep meaning and successful sexual relationships. Many women complain of their partners wanting to have sex with them with no foreplay. This leads to a lot of uncomfortable sexual relations. The way that men and women get sexually aroused is very different. Men are visual beings, so just the sight of their wife in beautiful lingerie will turn them on. While for women, it takes time to build up which needs to start in the mind. The mind needs to be aroused followed by the body before the actual sexual act. The Prophet of Islam (ﷺ) understood this clearly, he understood that it takes preparation to get the woman ready for sexual relations.

The Prophet Muhammad explained clearly; Anas ibn Malik (radiyallahu 'anhu) reports that Nabi (ﷺ) said:

> "*One of you should not fulfil one's sexual need from one's wife like an animal, rather there should be between them foreplay of kissing and words.*"

Author Habeeb Akande outlines in his book 'A Taste of Honey', the different forms of foreplay. He explains that there are 3 types of foreplay: mental, verbal and physical. He writes:

> "Mental foreplay, also known as mental stimulation, is the psychological and emotional stimulation that takes place to arouse sexual desire. Mental foreplay is a crucial component of the lovemaking experience, again most particularly for women."

He writes about verbal foreplay: "The Prophet (ﷺ) said "some eloquence is magic."

Verbal foreplay can be subtle or it can be direct. Sometimes sweet words are required, and at other times more explicit terms. A man who is well versed in verbal foreplay knows when to call his wife sexy and when to let her know she is beautiful. The importance of verbal foreplay in arousing a woman cannot be overemphasised.

Underlining its importance, the Prophet (ﷺ) told men to shower their wives with loving compliments prior to engaging in actual intercourse when he said, "one of you should not fulfil one's sexual need with ones wife like an animal, rather there should be between them foreplay of kissing and sweet words."

Habeeb carries on explaining about physical foreplay and writes:

> "Once a couple are psychologically prepared and in the mood for sex, they should proceed to physical foreplay. Physical foreplay includes all physical sexual acts short of actual penetration."

What we learn from what Habeeb outlined as the 3 forms of foreplay is that there is more to foreplay than just a quick kiss and a hug. It is important for couples, especially men, to understand the different types of foreplay and use them appropriately with their partner.

The Five Love Languages

The five love languages are five different ways of expressing and receiving love: words of affirmation, quality time, receiving gifts, acts of service, and physical touch. Not everyone communicates love in the same way, and likewise, people have different ways they prefer to receive love. The concept of love languages was developed by Gary Chapman, PhD., in his book 'The 5 Love Languages: The Secret to Love That Lasts', where he describes these five unique styles of communicating love, categories he distilled from his experience in marriage counselling and linguistics.

1. Words of affirmation

People with words of affirmation as a love language value verbal acknowledgments of affection, including frequent "I love you's," compliments, words of appreciation, verbal encouragement, and often frequent digital communication like texting and social media engagement. "Written and spoken shows of affection matter the most to these people," says couples' psychotherapist Fariha Mahmud-Syed. "These expressions make them feel understood and appreciated."

2. Quality time

People whose love language is quality time feel most adored when their partner actively wants to spend time with them and is always down to hang out. They particularly love when active listening, eye contact, and full presence are prioritised hallmarks in the relationship. "This love language is all about giving your undivided attention to that one special person, without the distraction of television, phone screens, or any other outside interference. They have a strong desire to actively spend time with their significant other, having meaningful conversations or sharing recreational activities," Mahmud-Syed says.

3. Acts of services

If your love language is acts of service, you value

when your partner goes out of their way to make your life easier. It's things like bringing you soup when you're sick, making your coffee for you in the morning, or picking up your dry cleaning for you when you've had a busy day at work. "This love language is for people who believe that actions speak louder than words. Unlike those who prefer to hear how much they're cared for, people on this list like to be shown how they're appreciated. Doing the smaller and bigger chores to make their lives easier or more comfortable is highly cherished by these folks," shares Mahmud-Syed.

4. Gifts

Gifts is a pretty straightforward love language: You feel loved when people give you "visual symbols of love," as Chapman calls it. It's not about the monetary value but the symbolic thought behind the item. People with this style recognize and value the gift-giving process: the careful reflection, the deliberate choosing of the object to represent the relationship, and the emotional benefits from receiving the present. "People whose love language is receiving gifts enjoy being gifted something that is both physical and meaningful. The key is to give meaningful things that matter to them and reflect their values, not necessarily yours," says Mahmud-Syed.

5. Physical touch

People with physical touch as their love language feel loved when they receive physical signs of affection, including kissing, holding hands, cuddling on the couch, and sex. Physical intimacy and touch can be incredibly affirming and serve as a powerful emotional connector for people with this love language. The roots go back to our childhood, Motamedi notes. Some people only felt deep affection and love from their parents when they were held, kissed, or touched. "People who communicate their appreciation through this language, when they consent to it, feel appreciated when they are hugged, kissed, or cuddled. They value the feeling of warmth and comfort that comes with physical touch," says Mahmud-Syed.

To know and understand the five languages is very important. This can bring a lot of beauty into the relationship. Once you know what your favourite love language is you can then communicate this important information to your partner. This will allow them to give you more of the love language that they like most. This is something that is a symbolic gesture, but extremely effective. It will also help you to have a deeper understanding and connection with your partner. For example, if your partner's favourite love language is acts of service, then make sure you regularly do acts of service for your partner, this will be really appreciated.

One point to add here is that relationships are fluid and need work. If you don't work on them they can become stale and stagnant, also everyone's relationship can improve. You will find that those with the best relationships are the couples that actively work on improving it. A good starting point on improving your relationship is by gaining more knowledge on what makes marriages successful.

Where to Look for A Spouse

In today's society it can be very difficult to find a spouse. We live in a society where everyone is so busy with work that it's difficult to find places to socialise. This is an issue for both Muslims and non-Muslims.

Social media has become a great resource where people are meeting each other. All of the platforms being used such as Facebook, Instagram, Twitter and now Clubhouse, are all platforms that Muslims are using to meet potential spouses. This is a far cry from the arranged marriage situation where parents would pick spouses for their children. Many of the people using these platforms are professional people that have successful careers, but have not really given thought on marriage and now feel they are getting older and need to take that plunge. A Buzzfeed article entitled, 'Muslims Are Defying Conventions By Falling In Love On Instagram', states online dating for Muslims is booming.

Shahzad Younas, who founded the UK-based Muzz (formerly named Muzmatch), which has been described as "Muslim Tinder", told BuzzFeed News that membership more than doubled between December 2015 and December 2016.

"We have had over 2,500 people tell us they left Muzmatch after finding someone on the app," said Younas. "We have heard back specifically on around 300-plus actual weddings so far around the world."

Yet romance on the internet is an issue with which my millennial Muslim friendship circle have a love-hate relationship. The problems are many and varied. The lack of decent guys. The issue of catfishing on dating apps. The goals of interracial Muslim couples. The seemingly ubiquitous habit of random guys sliding into DMs. The jokes about becoming a Muslim "Insta-couple" for the retweets. The incessant "How We Met" YouTube videos. And the biggest question of them all: How does one go about finding love in a halal way online anyway?

Dating online is seen by some as the solution to the much discussed "crisis of marriage", which is also referred to in some British Muslim circles as "the Muslim spinster crisis", explains Dr Fauzia Ahmad, a sociologist at Royal Holloway, University of London.

Many more women – who are often well-educated, professional, and older – attend Muslim marriage events than men.

"Getting married and staying married is one of the biggest contemporary issues facing Muslim diasporas," Ahmad writes in an article titled, 'British Muslims' relationship crisis' – "Yet it is an issue that many mosques, Muslim organisations, secular, legal and welfare services are failing to offer adequate support for."

BE PREPARED

Your partner may be anywhere in the world and you could meet them absolutely anywhere. Although we can list many places where you can find love, including social media or through friends, those places may not be where *you* find love. You may meet your partner anywhere; it could be in the gym or at the library. I'm not saying that when you go to those places that you wait to find love. But I want you to have awareness that your partner could be anywhere and you may meet them at the juice bar or shopping at Wholefoods.

Why is it important to be aware? I was talking to a sister about this same situation and she explained that when she was a little younger and still at university, there were many men that showed her great interest, but because her mind wasn't in that state, she wasn't aware that the brothers were showing her real interest. She only realised many years later when she reflected on the situation.

Always be open for the opportunity to arise. I have one of my good friends who had been looking to get married for years with no success. I will call him Ahmed just for this example. Ahmed had gotten to a situation where he had given up on the idea of ever finding his soul mate.

Then one day I was out with my wife and we met a lovely sister and my wife thought this would be a great partner for Ahmed. So I phoned him and told him about this lovely sister we had met and I thought that she would be an ideal partner for him. Because of all of the unsuccessful relationships that he had in the past he was reluctant to give it a try. When my wife heard this she got on the phone and explained to Ahmed that he should be open and give her a chance because she thought that they really suited. In the end he agreed to meet with her and now they have been happily married for over 10 years.

So you can see from this example that Allah can put your blessings anywhere and you have to be open and ready to receive the blessings. If Ahmed wasn't open to giving it one more try, he would never have had the opportunity to meet his lovely wife.

I find that when individuals are mentally ready to get married they usually get married quite soon. They create the environment around them that allows their other half to appear. Then on the other hand, I have met many brothers that say they are ready to get married but after working with them you soon realise that they are not fully prepared to get married. Their mouth may utter the words that they are ready, but you soon realise that their heart is not ready to take that step.

It's Not All Smooth Sailing

Every couple should be warned that marriage is not all smooth sailing. In today's society when things don't work we just throw them away, but remember with marriage it is two individuals who have journeyed together and spent time together; two people that have known each other intimately.

In marriage you will learn things about yourself that you didn't even know existed. Both you and your partner will have amazing, beautiful times together but you will also have testing times when you will hate each other.

Marriage takes resilience, patience, effort and swallowing your pride.

It is shocking that the person you love so dearly may turn around and hurt you so deeply it cuts like a knife. This is the reality of marriage, but to make it work you need to put that effort in.

Gary Chapman explains the reality of marriage in today's society for many.

He explains:

> "Ours has been called the "Throwaway Society." We buy our food in beautiful containers, which we then throw away. Our cars and tech devices quickly become obsolete. We give our furniture to the second-hand shop not because it is no longer functional, but because it is no longer in style. We even "throw away" unwanted pregnancies. We sustain business relationships only so long as they are profitable to the bottom line. Thus, it is no shock that our society has come to accept the concept of a "throwaway marriage." If you are no longer happy with your spouse, and your relationship has run on hard times, the easy thing is to abandon the relationship and start over."

This is exactly what many people do today in their relationships and as soon as they hit hard times they are out, they quit, throw in the towel.

But even to do that is not easy, there are a lot of emotions involved in that heart break. Chapman explains:

> "No one can walk away from a spouse as easily as he or she can sell bad stock. Indeed, talk to most adults who have chosen divorce as the answer, and you will find the divorce was preceded by months of intense inner struggle, and that the whole ordeal is still viewed as a deeply painful experience."

Please note, I'm not saying that nobody should get divorced. There are many sick people in this world who make life hell for their partners. To all of those who are in abusive relationships, I tell them to get out as soon as possible. Abuse has to be a limit whether it is physical, emotional, psychological or sexual. If you find yourself in an abusive relationship then I would advise you to leave. But there are many relationships that can be saved, one of the main causes in these kinds of situations is bad communication. This is a common issue in relationships where there are problems, but the good news is that it can be fixed with work from both individuals.

DIVORCE HAPPENS

What does Islam say about divorce and remarriage?

Divorce is something that is not liked by Allah, but it is allowed to happen. There is a hadith which explains that divorce rocks the throne of Allah; which means that Allah is not pleased with the separation of couples. But saying that, it is important to understand that it is allowed.

In today's society the amount of Muslims getting divorced is rising. There are many reasons for the rise of divorce including:

1- Physical, mental, or emotional abuse or torture: When one of the spouses becomes abusive and inflicts physical, mental, or emotional torture, and is not willing to change by taking practical measures through therapy or counselling, then it is a valid reason for seeking divorce, for the Islamic principle states, "There shall be no inflicting or receiving of harm." Zhulm (injustice) is not tolerated in Islam, regardless of who the perpetrator is.

2- Failure to fulfil the objectives and purposes for which marriage was initiated: This can be utter incompatibility between the partners, which may be expressed by their irreconcilable differences in temperaments, likes, and dislikes.

3- Marital infidelity: This can be a major cause for dissolution of marriage, for marriage is built on trust and confidence. Its main purpose is to preserve the chastity and modesty of those involved. Once this foundation is eroded and undermined and there is no chance to restore the same, then divorce is the way to go.

4- Failure of the husband to provide: When the man, who is considered the provider and maintainer of the family, fails to shoulder his responsibilities and the wife decides that she cannot continue tolerating his shirking of responsibility, this is grounds for divorce.

The Prophet Muhammad (ﷺ) cautioned against senseless exercise of divorce when he said, "Among lawful things, divorce is most hated by Allah." (Abu Dawud)

> "And if you have reason to fear that a breach might occur between a [married] couple, appoint an arbiter from among his people and an arbiter from among her people; if they both want to set things alright, God may bring about their reconciliation. Behold, God is indeed all-knowing, aware." (Qur'an, 4:35)

In other words, an arbiter from both sides would be appointed to resolve the differences and if the arbitration council fails to help the husband and wife reconcile their differences, then they can recommend the divorce, or if they have been given the authority to take a decision, they can pronounce and execute the divorce.

Although it is not encouraged, most Muslims agree that divorce is permitted if a marriage has broken down, and generally Muslims are permitted to remarry if they so wish. However, there are differences between Muslims about the procedures for divorce and remarriage:

- Sunni Muslims do not require witnesses. The husband must express his desire for a divorce on three separate occasions with a waiting period of three months.

- Shi'a Muslims require two witnesses, followed by a waiting period before a marriage can end.

- If a woman initiates a divorce it is called 'khula'. There must be a waiting period to ensure the woman is not pregnant.

Although Shari'ah Law permits divorce, in the hadith, Abdullah ibn Umar reported that the Prophet Muhammad (ﷺ) said the most detestable of lawful things before Allah is divorce. So although divorce is allowed, Muslims should try to avoid it, if possible. This means that many Muslims who experience marital difficulties will try to resolve their issues. It is also because they have made a contract before God, called a 'nikah', to remain together for life and divorce would mean breaking that contract.

Consequently, divorce has been generally frowned upon in Islam; hence it is imperative that we exhaust every possible avenue to avert the same; the steps thus recommended involve the following:

1- Seek counsel from those who possess wisdom, experience, and knowledge and seek to solve the outstanding issues between yourselves after gaining insight and advice from them.

2- In the event that such efforts fail, both spouses must resort to Islamic arbitration; in this arbitration one should have parties representing both sides. They should submit to abide by the decisions thus agreed upon.

The reason for this is that often humans become so preoccupied with their temporary personal likes and dislikes that they fail to see their own destructive behaviours and weaknesses. Thus they are encouraged to seek advice and wisdom from those with experience and knowledge, who may help them to empower themselves to take charge of rectifying their behaviour and attitudes.

LIFE AFTER DIVORCE

I have mentioned that divorce is disliked by Allah because it is the break up of relationships. But it is not the end of everything. In the West especially, divorces are happening more and more. This is because people now want different things out of their relationships and if their partner can not fulfil what they need, then they would rather go it alone.

One of the big challenges that Muslims need to think about is how they manage arranged marriages, especially when the marriage is with one person who is abroad. This raises many issues and conflicts especially if one person is born in the UK and one is born abroad. They have different life experiences and different expectations for their relationship. Many men from traditional backgrounds are expecting a traditional partner like what they see in their local village, but if they marry someone who is brought up in the West their experience and expectations are totally different. This leads to a lot of conflict and ultimately divorce.

CHALLENGE OF DIVORCE

In some Muslim cultures, for example in the Asian community, women that have been married are shunned. In the UK, we have a large proportion of Asian Muslim women who have been married and now are divorced who never get married again.

That is because a lot of the men in that culture are looking for a younger woman who is a virgin to marry, this is the case even when the man has been married before.

In other Muslim communities, such as in the Somali or Mauritanian community, you find that women who have been divorced before have no problem re-marrying. In the Mauritanian community especially, it is celebrated when a woman is divorced. It means she is available for marriage, and experienced, which attracts men to marry them.

DIVORCE WITH RESPECT

Rayesa, who is a divorce life coach, explains that when she was getting divorced she had a divorce coach who helped her through this tough situation. Divorce is an emotionally charged time, it is when the bubble has been broken, the dream turned into a nightmare. At this time emotions are usually running very high and ex-partners are fed up with their ex and in some cases, just want to see the back of them. But even though this is the case we must try our best to separate with respect.

"Divorce can be something that we are rewarded for if we do it in a manner that is pleasing to Allah", explains Rayesa. This is a great idea because Allah always wants us to be our best in every situation. Even if it is the most challenging for you, it's still important to treat other people with respect.

HOW TO SOLVE POSSIBLE CHALLENGES

When things are not going right in a marriage, the first thing to do is sit down with your partner and talk about the issues that are affecting the relationship in a negative way. Sometimes this can have a positive result and resolve the problem. I would always advise to start there; communication is a powerful tool and can rectify many misunderstandings and wrong actions.

If that doesn't rectify the situation then seek help.

Depending on what the situation is, that will help to negotiate matters; whether you need professional advice or advice from a family member, both are positive steps.

Make sure you talk to someone about the situation; it's important that you don't carry on suffering in silence. There are so many people that can help in whatever situation you find yourself in. The first task is to start searching.

Dr. Aneesah Nadir talks about the importance of premarital reasons to discuss everything about each other and to get to know each other. It's important that if there are underlying issues, like mental or physical ill health, these should be explained and spoken about well before a marriage happens. This allows an individual to make the decision if he/she wants to proceed or not. She states:

> "Marriage frequently brings together individuals who have physical and mental health problems. In most cases, these matters are not discussed prior to marriage thereby impeding the couple's ability to weather a chronic condition like asthma, diabetes, hypertension or

a catastrophic event such as injury due to accident or major illness.

Whether a spouse suffers from a physical condition or chronic mental illness, premarital conversation concerning the nature of the disorder, medications used and effective reaction to episodic flare-ups must be engaged in order to prepare the couple for inherent challenges of living with and caring for a sick spouse."

Dr. Nadir makes a serious point here. When planning to get married it's important to know everything about the person, or as much as you can.

I know of an incident where a couple got married and then the wife fell sick a few months after and this sickness has lasted for years. This put the husband in a very difficult situation because he had just entered into a marriage and before he had a real chance to know his wife she had fallen ill. Of course, we could argue that this is his test from Allah and that is a good argument, but it's also important for you to do your due research before entering into any agreement.

It would also be very important to understand the mental health of the individual, because if they are suffering from severe mental health this is very important and the potential spouse has a right to know what he/she is getting involved with.

There have been many high profile cases of women marrying dangerous men who start off nice but soon after start physically abusing their wife and in the most detrimental cases the wife has lost her life.

In one case, it was found in court that the man had a history of violence and had already been to prison before for violently attacking someone. This information was purposely withheld from the wife so that she would marry him, which is wrong. The woman and the man have the right to know who they are getting married to.

Mastering Male and Female Energies

Every human has both male and female energies in them. The best relationships happen when there is a balance of both energies in both people. When the balance of male and female energies are present in both individuals, this leads to deeper and richer relationships.

Bonnie Sadigh explains this very well in her article, 'The Power of Energies':

> "If we understand the underlying energetic dynamic of our relationship and work towards balancing both our masculine and feminine energies; we can be guaranteed a much healthier and prosperous relationship.
>
> Masculine and feminine energy have

nothing do with gender, we all have both energies within us. Typically, men tend to have more masculine energy and less of feminine energy and women usually have more feminine energy than masculine. Although this can be totally reversed as well".

The way we are socially conditioned means we grow up following certain gender roles which are extremely restrictive. We are taught that a boy should act in a certain way and that girls should act in a certain way. This does not allow the individuals to get in touch with their opposite energies. Bonnie goes on to explain this:

"However, because of our upbringing and culture, we were taught that you are either a male or a female. So if you were a boy and you cried, you were most probably labelled as a sissy or heard something along the lines of "STOP IT, boys don't cry!" Or if you were a girl, and liked to play with trucks and enjoyed digging in the dirt rather than playing with dolls, you were labelled as a tomboy."

We have learnt more about the individual self. Today we have a better understanding about the different energies that we have inside us. The fact is that society has separated the two for thousands of years. We were never taught about how a female should approach her masculine side, or a male approaching his feminine side in balance.

Characteristically, we were taught that we are either male or female with no mention or validation of the fact that everyone has both aspects in their core makeup.

For any relationship to succeed, and for personal growth and fulfilment, both partners need to be in touch with their less dominant energies.

A balance between the two energies is what makes us whole and sustains a healthy relationship. The masculine and the feminine energies are like the poles of a magnet. Depending on where you are energetically on this pole determines what kind of a relationship you have; whether you complement each other or continuously argue and butt heads.

If you are entirely on the opposite side of the

pole; meaning the masculine energy is at its highest and the feminine on the opposite side at its highest, (extreme masculine and extreme feminine) what you probably have is a lot of chemistry, fiery passion, and sexual attraction, but not a whole lot of deep and meaningful conversation.

If the energies are close to each other toward the centre of the pole, you probably have a good, stable relationship with deep and meaningful connections. The imbalance happens when the energies fall into the same side of the pole.

Most conflicts arise when both partners demonstrate dominant masculine energies in a relationship. This creates a constant power struggle between the two partners. Both want to be in charge, both want to be the decision-makers, and both want to have things their way!

The most stagnant relationship comes from two feminine dominant energy partners where neither is comfortable in taking charge or making sound decisions. It is when relationships get boring; there is no adventure, no excitement, and nothing of significance is happening.

If a female has more masculine energy, she thrives

with a partner that is in touch with his feminine energy. Males with feminine energy respect and are comfortable with their partners being in the workforce, being in charge, and having a direction in their lives.

On the contrary, females that demonstrate more of a feminine energy are content with a masculine energy male to take control and be the dominant breadwinner and the decision-maker.

Understanding energies and how they can enhance your relationship comes down to one word: BALANCE; where both men and women are in touch with their core energies and trust their partner's core energy and are ok with displaying their less dominant energy when appropriate. It becomes a sort of a dance when sometimes the man leads, and the woman follows, and sometimes the woman leads, and the man follows. It is getting into that perfect Yin and yang –where two pieces of a puzzle fit into each other perfectly.

Now let's discuss the characteristics of each energy.

MASCULINE ENERGY- FIRE

Masculine energy is all about taking action, loves to build and loves to fix things. Masculine sees a problem and immediately wants to fix it. It's protective. Most women are looking for a partner to protect them, they want to feel safe, and they are looking for the energy of protection. Masculine energy is strong and stable. It's self-confident.

Masculine energy likes to make decisions fast. It's decisive. Knows what it wants and goes after getting it. Masculine energy loves direction and a purpose. It's competitive and likes to win and break through barriers. It's logical.

Masculine energy uses words more than emotions, and doesn't hold on to things. Whether emotion or tangible things, it can let go very quickly.

It seeks freedom. Masculine energy loves to be free. It loves acknowledgement. Masculine energy craves importance; they love it when they are given a compliment. They want to be heroes.

Masculine energy is independent and analytical, representing our left brain. When masculine energy is appropriately used, it is creative, practical, and visionary. When masculine energy is misused, it can end in ego, anger, resentment, and have inner conflict.

FEMININE ENERGY- WATER

Feminine energy, on the other hand, is vastly different. Different doesn't mean good or bad; it simply means different! Feminine energy is creative and inspiring – it's the energy that creates life. It loves beauty and it stimulates creativity. It's nurturing, it's supportive, it desires love and craves to receive love to feel fulfilled.

The feminine energy is intuitive and empathic. The feminine energy is fluid, stormy, emotional, passionate, and it flows from moment to moment like the waters of a river. Feminine energy craves adoration, they love to be admired and appreciated. Nothing lights up feminine energy more than to give her a compliment.

Feminine energy is intelligent and loving and contains the quality of our compassion, emotion, empathy, and truth. When you are strong in your feminine energy, you have a strong connection to your body and intuition, and you can make decisions based on what you feel in your heart. Feminine energy is receptive, right-brained energy. Yet, if we are too much in our feminine, we can come across as weak and lose our personal power.

Masculine and Feminine energies are both equally important and necessary. To be balanced, to get things done, and to have a healthy relationship, both the masculine and the feminine need to be present. We just need to realise when and how much of each energy is necessary. The key is BALANCE; a dance between the two and knowing where and when to use each.

Benefits and Dangers of Social Media

In her dissertation, Aysha Ahmed quotes a piece from the Economist. It states that:

> "Muslim youngsters are adopting technology to distance themselves from older, traditional practices while also challenging Western models." (Economist, 2012)

Since the rise of globalisation, Muslims have been changing their behaviour when it comes to dating and looking for spouses. If we go back 20 years, one of the main ways that Muslims would get married would be through arranged marriage. That would happen by family members sourcing a spouse for their son or daughter. Sometimes this would work out fine but now, in many cases, young people who are looking to get married are taking the task on themselves and are going online to find love.

Abrar Al-Heeti in her article on Cnet.com entitled, 'Beyond Tinder: How Muslim Millennials are Looking for Love', writes:

> "We're the generation that was born with the rise of technology and social media," says Mariam Bahawdory, founder of Muslim dating app Eshq, which, similar to Bumble, allows women to make the first move. "It's not like we can go to clubs or bars to meet people in our community, because there's a reputation to uphold and there's a stigma attached to going out and meeting people."

Young Muslims are embracing the new technologies with both hands and are independently going out to find love. This has come with its own set of challenges. Sometimes the parents don't agree with the person their son or daughter brings home. This could be because they are the wrong colour and come from a different tribe or sect of Islam.

As young Muslims are ready to embrace the new globalised Islamic world they see in front of them, oftentimes their parents are not and are stuck in their old ways.

Mona Alyedreessy writes in her book entitled, 'The Muslim Narcissist':

> "The rapid growth of social media and dating and marriage apps have created a generation of people who hide behind screens and book dates like they'd ordered food."

This shows how computerised and easy it has become to meet people; just by clicking on a button, there are all of these opportunities in front of you.

She continues:

> "While instant communication apps and dating apps have their advantages, they've caused most people to lose the beauty of human connection, innocent love and genuine relationships. Now our options for partners pop up on our screens every day, like a robotic catalogue of emotionless faces that

we're to swipe left or right on, judging them primarily by their profile picture. Before you know it, you're talking to seven or eight people at once, which is a very confusing and time consuming process and a great distraction from more important things in life."

She raises some interesting points which include the idea that it is very easy to be talking to multiple people at the same time. Islamically this is wrong, as you should really only be talking to one person at a time. When you do this it allows you to give all of your focus and attention to that one person. Talking to multiple people at the same time is a confusing place to be in, you will not be able to focus fully because you will have so much choice.

CHALLENGES OF SOCIAL MEDIA

There are multiple challenges on social media and it's important for sincere individuals to be aware of the challenges that surround using the internet to find love.

There are many insincere people on the internet. One of the problems with the internet is that everyone can easily get onto it. Access to it is available to most people around the globe. This can be challenging because both good and bad have the same access. Some people you meet online are not really interested in marriage but just want to have a sexual relationship.

Unfortunately, there are men out there that prey on innocent Muslimahs, enticing them by using beautiful words and giving them gifts with the real aim of only sleeping with them. Once they have done that they will drop the sister and move on to find their next victim.

The way for Muslim sisters to protect themselves from this happening is to first let others be aware that you are talking to someone. Seek guidance on every step from respectable people that you trust. It is also advisable to not meet the person on your own, especially in a private room or space.

SOME PEOPLE ARE NOT WHAT THEY SEEM

It's very easy to create a fake profile, even school children are very proficient at doing this. Definitely check out who you are talking to, make sure they are the person in the photo.

BACK UP CHECKS ARE NEEDED

This will mean family members investigating the potential spouse. This is usually done by the potential spouse giving information or references to people who can vouch for their character and personality. In today's society there are many narcissists around and unfortunately many of them are prevalent on social media and especially on marriage apps. They use these apps as a place to hunt or seek out their next victim. Inform your loved ones if you want to pursue someone.

BENEFITS OF PRE-MARITAL COACHING AND COUNSELLING

We are living in a very different society than the one our parents inherited. Relationships are becoming more complex, so issues around marriage are also developing. Therefore, it's important that couples that are getting ready to embark on the journey of marriage prepare themselves. This can be done by organising meetings with a relationship coach or marriage counsellor.

In every partnership you go into it's normal to get training in that area, so you know what to expect and how to operate in this new setting. That's why it's so strange that when it comes to marriage there is not enough pre-work done. You will find that the people that spend time preparing before the marriage will have a smoother relationship. It doesn't mean that if you don't do any pre-work your relationship will fail, but it does mean that if you do some work beforehand this will benefit your relationship.

In an article entitled, 'Premarital Counselling: Is It Right for You?' by Sanjana Gupta, she talks about the benefits of pre-marital counselling:

> "Pre-marriage counselling is for couples who are planning to marry and may wish to resolve any issues they have before the marriage. This practice was formerly relegated to certain religious factions; however, more secular couples are engaging in premarital counselling. Many studies have been conducted in order to understand the benefits of attending pre-marriage counselling."

There are many couples whose relationships fail because of miscommunication. Even if the two of you think you know each other, miscommunications can happen. Any person can misinterpret what you say and think you have ill intent. Or you may want your partner to do something, but the communication just isn't working.

Some people think their needs are being expressed, but they aren't communicating them well enough, and then they get upset when miscommunications happen. No matter what the reason, miscommunications will happen, but premarital counselling can help reduce them and teach you how to resolve miscommunication.

Pre-marriage counselling teaches you how to talk to your partner and express your needs. It's also a great place to help understand the root of the conflicts that are happening. Sitting down with a pre-marital counsellor can encourage you to analyse what causes the issues, and what you can do to prevent them. It gives the couples a chance to learn how to communicate better, and use conflict resolution skills that will make their life easier.

The millennial generation has large issues around communicating. They talk a lot through social media, but that's not the same as talking face to face.

In an article in Bustle, an online magazine, it states that one of the issues that Millennials have is communication:

> "Because so many millennials rely on texting to have conversations, experts say they tend to have in-person communication problems."

A common thread throughout many of these conflicts is that couples don't know how to communicate their needs and desires to their partner. Clinical psychologist Dr. Ryan Hooper says, "They are communicating a ton of information to each other through social media and texting, but many of the most important things are going unsaid." While this may not always be the case, if you are finding it difficult to communicate with your partner in person, remember that more heavy conversations should be handled face-to-face rather than over text. There was one case where a man ended his relationship over text, which is really unacceptable. When a relationship breaks up this can be very traumatic and to just end the relationship by text is insensitive to say the least. It shows a lack of respect for the other person and maybe also a fear of dealing with uncomfortable situations. When a relationship is going to end, both parties should have an understanding of why the relationship ended.

It is said by psychologists that around 70% of your communication is non-verbal. So where millennials are so strong on texting, they are missing out on body language and a great deal of powerful and deep conversations where they can spread meaning and understanding.

Another issue can be phone use, when the partner is on the phone too much and is not paying attention to their spouse. This is called "phubbing". This is a real issue with millennials. Carina Wolff explains about it in her article on Bubble:

> "Phubbing" is when a person snubs their partner by being on their phone instead of interacting." "Couples are focusing on other things and ignoring their partners when they are together," says Mutchler. "It sends a message that the partner is not the most important thing in the moment — that we'd rather focus on something else."

The solution? Create no-phone guidelines within your relationship. For example, if it's date night, keep the phone in pockets or bags to make sure you both remain present in the moment.

In an article entitled, 'Your Partner's Dependency On Their Phone Is Hurting You More Than You Think' by Lea Rose Emery, Emery writes about the feeling of being excluded by phubbing:

> "Although they found that phubbing was bad for, well, pretty much everything, the results noted that it had a particularly negative impact on "the need to belong". It's not really a surprise, because phubbing has a way of making you feel immediately left out. And, as the study authors pointed out, phubbing is different to other forms of social exclusion and isolation because it can be done so easily — and pretty much anywhere."

Phubbing is something that can be done so easily without the understanding of the negative impact it can cause. I have been out with my wife when she has told me clearly to put my phone away so that we can enjoy some private time together.

In her article, Carina talks about cheating in relationships and how social media is also to blame for making it much easier to cheat. This happened through the creation of many apps, which makes it easier to cheat and also to hide the infidelity.

Coaching can benefit a couple who are preparing to get married by helping them get prepared for what is to come. For example, living together with another person 24-7 is very different from living with your parents or even flat sharing.

Coaching can give you a deep understanding about the whole experience of marriage and what to expect. I ran a four day workshop entitled, 'Getting Ready for Love', and one piece of the feedback I received was:

> "I enjoyed your course so much and it really opened my eyes to marriage and what it entails. You have given me lots to think about when preparing for marriage."

Mindset Shift

The way we think about our own relationships and our partner matters. As a relationship develops, people develop beliefs about themselves, their partner, and the relationship. These beliefs influence the way we act within the relationship, how much motivation we feel, how vulnerable and open we can be, and how flexible we are willing to be.

When we enter a relationship with a positive view on things, this will benefit the relationship in the long run. People with a growth mindset are the ones that feel optimistic about relationships.

They believe that things can improve and the way to do that is to put the effort in and work at it. People with a growth mindset believe that knowledge is key.

So to improve anything, it's important that you first go and learn about it. Once this has been achieved you can use the keys you have learnt to improve.

In her book, 'Mindset: The New Psychology of Success', Carol Dweck shares two mindsets that impact our relationships.

The first is the fixed mindset, or believing things are set in stone and cannot be changed. This might mean we believe that our partner's qualities cannot be changed or that the relationship's qualities cannot be developed. "In the fixed mindset," she writes, "The ideal is instant, perfect, and perpetual compatibility."

The second is the growth mindset. This is the belief that with work, focus, and practice, our skills can be developed and changed over time.

Someone with a fixed mindset might say, "They should know what makes me feel loved!" Whereas a person with a growth mindset says, "I believe my partner can learn how to love me if I communicate clearly and they work hard at it."

Or a fixed-mindset individual says, "I shouldn't have to work on my relationship. If it isn't good now, it will never be good." A growth-mindset person would say, "Relationships go through periods of highs and lows. I think we can get through this if we both make a consistent effort."

THE 5 STAGES OF MARRIAGE

All marital unions, more or less, go through some predictable stages. Most people understand that relationships grow and change over time. There are specific, defined stages of long-term relationships, which offer new feelings, new challenges to overcome, and new opportunities for growth. Every couple will move through these stages at different speeds, and most people will experience each stage more than once – it is common to fluctuate from one stage to another. Hence, most marriages will cover these stages maybe once or more.

These are the important stages of marriage a couple goes through:

1. The Honeymoon Stage
Usually, the first year or two is a passion-fuelled period that's all about the two of you and your intense focus on the attraction that made you want to walk down the aisle to

begin with. It's the initial, sweeping romance that often consumes a couple when they first get together.

2. Settling In, Settling Down

The second stage of marriage takes place as the first comes to an end – sometimes gradually, at other times suddenly, depending on the circumstances affecting the bride, groom and their life together. It's the realisation stage, during which you learn things you might not have known (or happily ignored) about your spouse's strengths, weaknesses and personal habits.

3. Disillusionment

The third stage of a relationship is the disillusionment stage. This is the winter season of love, one that may feel like the end of the road for some couples. At this point, the power struggles in the relationship have come fully to the surface; the issues the couple have consistently shoved under the rug are now glaringly obvious. Too many couples start to wonder: is this all there is to life?

4. The Safe Net

In this stage of marriage, husbands and wives begin to realise they married someone with as many vices as virtues, and each one reverts to re-inventing themselves in new ways. In the best scenario, this stage is about a reunion where you are getting to know each other all over again, unpacking old baggage and having fun.

5. Whole-Hearted Again

When the relationship is at its healthiest and most rewarding – couples experience true individuation, self-discovery, and the acceptance of imperfection in both themselves and their partners, recognising there is no such thing as a perfect match.

RISK TAKING

Part of marriage is risk taking, because you don't know all of the truth about an individual.

Unfortunately, in this world that we live in, many times people lie to hide the reality of the person who wants to get married. This is done so that the person will not be put off by their potential spouse but this is against the teachings of Islam. It is important that you tell the 100% truth about a person who wants to get married and do not hide anything even if it is bad.

This is very important because if you don't, you are misleading the person who wants to get married and when the person finds out, they may end the marriage out of anger and being deceived. They have a right to know all of the facts about a person before they get married to them. Then they can make a choice based on all of the facts.

Many people try to hide medical conditions such as mental health, heart conditions, blood conditions, if they are able to have children and so forth. It's important to tell them all of the facts.

Dr. Nadir states that we need to move towards a strong movement which respects marriage and makes sure it is done correctly. She writes:

> "I believe we all need to join the healthy marriage movement in the larger

society and promote it within our own Muslim communities. Because marriage is the primary unit and cornerstone of society, we need to focus on it. The time is now to end drive-by nikahs and spontaneous marriage ceremonies in the imams office just after Friday prayers. The time is now to put an end to quickie marriage ceremonies with a wali and witnesses who don't know the bride and groom."

We have to remember that the foundation of Islam is the family and the core of the family is the married couple. If they are not stable they will not be able to bring into the world well-adjusted individuals who will be good Muslims and also good human beings who will benefit society and the wider world.

THE IMPORTANCE OF GETTING MARRIED

It is clear that the Prophet Muhammad (ﷺ) saw marriage as one of the most important actions a Muslim could take part in. It's interesting because we also know that marriage is a struggle where you need to be able to get on with another person peacefully, where you grow together with another person in love and compassion, where you and your chosen partner work together on the path of Allah raising children to also be lovers of Islam, Qur'an and the Sunna of the Prophet Muhammad (ﷺ).

In the section on marriage, Imam Ghazali writes in his book, 'The Revival of the Religious Sciences', that the Prophet (ﷺ) loved marriage, and he used these hadiths to make this point clear:

> As for the akhbar, we have his [the Prophet's] (ﷺ) sayings: "Marriage is of my Sunnah; whoever refrains from my Sunnah refrains from me"; and he also said: "Marriage is of my Sunnah; whoever likes my fitrah (natural disposition)', let him follow my Sunnah."

All of the Prophet Muhammad's (ﷺ) life examples are good; whichever ones you introduce into your life, you will be blessed for it and marriage is one of them.

Imam Ghazali also brought evidence from the companions of the Prophet (ﷺ) who stressed the importance of getting married:

> "Ibn 'Abbas said, "The asceticism of an ascetic is not complete until he marries." It is possible that he considered marriage an act of devotion which renders asceticism perfect; but it seems that he meant to say thereby that the heart would not be safe from being overcome by desire except through marriage, and that asceticism is not perfect without emptying (faragh) the heart [of all preoccupations]. For that reason he would gather his young bondsmen (ghilman), Akramah and Kurayb and others reaching adulthood, and would say, "If you wish to get married, I will get you married; for when a slave commits adultery, he removes faith from his heart.""

It states clearly here that marriage is also a shield for committing haram acts. Living in Western societies, having casual relationships is seen as the norm, so to have sex outside of marriage is not a problem. But for a muslim it is a sin that should not be committed. That is enough reason to seek marriage as soon as you are in a good situation to commit to another human being.

Ibn Masud used to say, "Were there but ten days left of my life, I would be inclined to get married so as not to meet God a celibate."

This hadith of ibn Masud stresses the importance of marriage. It shows the companions of the Prophet (ﷺ) saw marriage as a must at all times:

> "Two of Mu'adh Ibn Jabal's wives died from the plague, and he, too, was afflicted with the plague; so he said, "Get me married, for I would not like to meet God a celibate." And this coming from both of them indicates that they considered marriage a virtue rather than a defence against the excessiveness of desire."

My Personal Insight Into Marriage

Marriage can be great and is a blessed Sunna of the Prophet Muhammad (ﷺ) . I was blessed by Allah to meet an amazing woman who I love dearly, who has given me 4 amazing children who are all very different from each other but are all wonderful, mash Allah.

I have been married for over 30 years, and in that time we have had our ups and downs but we have managed to get through it. One of the most important things is that we understand our journey. We understand that we are on this earth for a period and then we return back to Allah. This has helped us to put things in perspective.

Being able to forgive is an invaluable quality that all couples need. No one is perfect, but when you are able to forgive that means you will have a much stronger relationship that will be able to manage the tests that happen in every relationship.

With all the due diligence you do before marriage, you will not know everything about the individual; you will learn more when you are living together. That is why a part of marriage is reliance on Allah – you do your investigation then leave the rest to Him (SWT).

Remember, when looking for a partner some people are not who they say they are. Unfortunately, we do have hypocrites and liars amongst us. So sometimes people say one thing to you, but when you are living together you find out the reality which is the complete opposite.

After you are married try to set a period of about two years before having children. This will give you time to travel together and spend time really getting to know each other. This is key because when children come along it becomes more complicated dealing with problems because now there are other bodies involved in the relationship, and if you are married to a narcissist you may have to be connected to that person for life because of the children.

Try and gain knowledge about marriage and relationships. Read books which explain in detail the experience of living together. Learn about what happens after the marriage day. So much money is spent on these extravagant marriages with no time spent on how to live successfully with another human being.

Learn about sexual relationships between husband and wife. There are now good books written on sexual relationships. This is an important part of relationships as there are many relationships where sex is a massive issue. Lots of relationships also end because of lack of sex in the relationship. Sex is not anything to be ashamed of and in Muslim marriages there is a lot of it taking place, the evidence of this is the large families that we have in the Muslim community.

Sex is first to bring beautiful children into this earth, but it is also for pleasure when done in marriage; it's a sacred action where you are blessed by Allah for participating in it and pleasing your partner.

Communication, communication, communication! Every good partnership is based on good communication. Each person in the marriage needs to feel heard and respected and understood. This can only take place when the communication is clear and understood. The biggest challenge in relationships is poor communication. A large proportion of marriages end in divorce because of poor communication.

When you are introduced to someone for marriage take your time and get to know the person. Sometimes people are pushing you into marriage before you have had a chance to do your research into the person. Take your time, there is no hurry, it's better you take your time and get the right partner.

THE PROPHET (ﷺ) AND HIS WIVES

As Muslims, we take our example from the Prophet Muhammad (ﷺ). So when we want to learn about relationships, it's important that we must spend some time reflecting on the best of creation and how he treated his womenfolk.

The Prophet (ﷺ) loved marriage: he said clearly that whoever does not run towards marriage is not of him. In his time, his companions followed his teachings to the letter but in today's society there are many Muslims who do not rush towards marriage, there are many that are dragging their feet.

Abu Hurairah narrated that The Messenger of Allah (ﷺ) said:

> "*The most complete of the believers in faith, is the one with the best character among them. And the best of you are those who are best to your women.*"

This also shows that being good to your partner is to be complete in faith, so we should strive to be good to our partners and make them happy.

I always say that if you want to know how someone really is, you must ask their partner. Because sometimes someone can be great outside or even a public speaker or community leader but at home they are a tyrant. This is totally wrong. Being just and fair to your family is part of religion.

Here are a few tips to keep your wife happy, contented and satisfied, just how our Prophet (ﷺ) did, with his Sunna ways.

1. Be kind and generous to your wife

The Prophet (ﷺ) treated all his wives equally and with utmost respect. He catered to their needs and always kept them above himself. He never hesitated to show how much value they held in his life. Show her her real importance and always treat her with kindness. Be gentle, kind and caring towards the women of the house.

2. Acknowledge her efforts

He (ﷺ) always appreciated even the littlest of things that his wives did for him, from cooking, to taking care of the children. He never took his wives' efforts for granted and showered them with respect and gratitude. Be grateful to Allah (SWT) for her, and to her for all her efforts. Appreciate her companionship and show her the same support.

3. Help her with daily chores

Prophet Muhammad (ﷺ) always supported his wives and helped them in household chores. He did his own work and even helped in cooking and cleaning the house. Don't let this be the duty of just the wives, help them out whenever you can and in whichever way you can. Work together to maintain and build your home. Allah (SWT) rewards the man who helps his wife in household chores.

4. Pray with her and pray for her

Our Prophet (ﷺ) has put a lot of emphasis on praying together. It is the duty of the husband to lead his wife in prayer. Gain blessings from Allah (SWT) together so that you can be in Jannah together. Engage in praying for her alone. Thank Allah (SWT) for her, and pray for her health and wellness always.

5. Surprise her with gifts

Gifts act as a token of appreciation in a relationship. It need not be materialistic gifts but any form of additional efforts shown by you. Cook food for her, get what she wants without her having to ask first, surprise her with random gifts, feed her with your own hands. All that is spent by a man on his wife, parents and children is a form of charity, which shall be rewarded. The Prophet Muhammad (ﷺ) used to feed Aisha (RA) with his own hands to express his love towards her.

6. Spend quality time with her

Spending time with your other half is the best way to get to know her better. It builds companionship, and to know about her needs and wants. Prophet Muhammad (ﷺ) not only talked to his wives, but also played halal fun games with them like horse riding. He made them feel close to him by devoting his time and attention to them. Allah puts barakah in the time you spend together.

7. Engage in sweet talks and gestures

Prophet Muhammad (ﷺ) never used to raise a voice at his wives. He was always gentle with them. He called them with sweet nicknames to make them feel special like 'Humaira' for Aisha (RA) (which means girl of reddish complexion). He often showed them gestures of love and affection like kissing them on the forehead while leaving and entering the house.

8. Listen to her attentively

Be there for your wife whenever she needs you. Listen to her when she opens up to you whether she's sad or excited. Listen to her like you actually care about what she shares with you and encourage her to share more. Our Prophet (ﷺ) always used to engage himself in conversations with his wives to make them feel important. He always acted like a friend in whom they could confide in.

9. Treat her with mercy

Prophet Muhammad (ﷺ) focused on forgiveness all through his life. He forgave people who were impossible to forgive. He (ﷺ) emphasised on treating wives well, with kindness and mercy whenever they made a mistake. He (ﷺ) was never rash and always overlooked their mistakes in public, while correcting them in private sweetly.

10. Make her feel secure

The responsibility of a woman comes under the man when she marries him. It is his duty to protect her and make her feel secure at all times. Always act like a door that can be opened by her whenever she's in trouble.

ACKNOWLEDGEMENTS

In the name of Allah, the Most Gracious, the Most Merciful. My gratitude above all is due to Allah for blessing me with the ability to write this book. I send endless salaams on our blessed messenger, Prophet Muhammed (SAW), the greatest example of love for humanity. I send praise and salaams on our blessed master, Sidna Sheikh Ahmed Tijani (RTA), and our master Sheikh Ibrahim Niass (RTA). I thank my Sheikh, Imam Cheikh Tidiane Cisse (RTA), for his continuous guidance and spiritual nourishment. To my dear wife, Amina, thank you for your endless support in all my endeavours and in reading and organising this text. Thank you, Sheikh Ibrahim Khaleel and Saida Aisha Cisse, for your guidance over the years. Thank you, Shaykh Ahmed Babikr and the Rumi's Cave community, for your sustained encouragement. I am in gratitude to all of my community, my dear friends and wonderful family. Sajida Mohammed, thank you for proofreading and organising the book, you have been invaluable. I extend my heartfelt gratitude to Habeeb Akande, Sekina Yakub, Dr. Mona Alyedreessy, Nazra Zuhyle, and my lovely daughter, Rakaya Fetuga, for reading the book before publication and offering your insights. Marko Joensuu, thank you for your work in publishing this book. I am grateful to everyone who has encouraged me in the process of writing this book, everyone who has purchased a copy and is benefitting from it. May Allah make it a source of guidance and support for all those who are seeking to get married, those who are married, and those who are divorced but have not given up on love.

Ameen.

BIBLIOGRAPHY

- Akande, H., 2015. A Taste of Honey: Sexuality and Erotology in Islam. London: Rabaah Publishers.
- Chapman, G., 1995. The 5 Love Languages: The Secret to Love That Lasts. Chicago: Northfield Publishing.
- Chapman, G., 2010. Things I Wish I'd Known Before We Got Married. Chicago: Northfield Publishing.
- Chapman, G., 2018, Loving Your Spouse When You Feel Like Walking Away, Chicago: Northfield Publishing.
- Emery, L.R., "Your Partner's Dependency On Their Phone Is Hurting You More Than You Think".
- Gupta, S., 2023. "Premarital Counselling: Is It Right for You?", verywellmind.com, Available at: https://www.verywellmind.com/premarital-counseling-definition-types-techniques-and-efficacy-5189767. Accessed, 2024.
- Kaley, N., Kaley, K., "Do Your Own Inner Work (The Secret to a Happy Marriage)", 2021, https://www.8080marriage.com/blog/Do-Your-Own-Inner-Work-The-Secret-to-a-Happy-Marriage. Accessed, 2024.
- Mojaddidi, H., "Emotional Intelligence Personified: How Following the Sunnah Can Save Your Marriage", almedina.org, 2017. Available at: https://www.almadina.org/studio/articles/emotional-intelligence-personified-how-following-the-sunnah-can-save-your-marriage. Accessed, 2024.
- ML. Mohammed., S., based on the book of the same name by Mufti Muhammad Ibn Adam Al-Kawthari, "Guidelines to Intimacy in Islam", Available at: https://irp-cdn.multiscreensite.com/3844bd1d/files/uploaded/Guidelines%20to%20intimacy%20in%20Islam%20pdf.pdf. Accessed, 2024.
- Nadir, A., "Preparing Muslims for Marriage", SoundVision, 2010, Available at: https://www.soundvision.com/article/preparing-muslims-for-marriage. Accessed, 2024.

- Roberts, N., Show Up: A motivational Message for Muslim Women, 2021, Liecestershire: Kube Publishing.
- Ruiz, D.M. and Mills, J., 1997. The Four Agreements: A Practical Guide To Personal Freedom. San Rafael, California: Amber-Allen Publishing.
- Sadigh, B., The Power of Energies.
- "Third Eye Open Interview with Rakin Niass", Interview With Divorce Coach Rayesa, 2021.
- Walid, D., 2017. 'Interracial' Marriage in the Prophetic Era, almadina. org, 20 November, Available at: https://www.almadina.org/studio/articles/interracial-marriage-in-the-prophetic-era. Accessed 2024.
- Wolff, C., "9 Relationship Problems Millennials Face The Most Of Any Age Group, According To Therapists", Bustle Magazine, 2018, Available at: https://www.bustle.com/p/9-relationship-problems-millennials-face-the-most-of-any-age-group-according-to-therapists-8082728. Accessed: 2024.